Poems
of
CONVICTION

Robert Greer

19ᵗʰ DEC 2020

To CAROLINE

JUST A SMALL GIFT TO SHOW MY
APPRECIATION TO YOU FOR ALL
YOUR PRAYERS, LOVE AND KINDNESS
TO ME OVER THIS PAST YEAR
WHICH HAS NOT BEEN AN EASY
YEAR FOR ME ARE ANYONE.
      YOUR FRIEND IN CHRIST
      GEORGE XX

GOD BLESS YOU IN 2021

Poems
of
CONVICTION

Volume 6

BOBBIE GREER

To order additional copies of this book, contact:
Xlibris
800-056-3182
www.Xlibrispublishing.co.uk
Orders@Xlibrispublishing.co.uk
809878

CONTENTS

DIFFERENCES

Each and every one of us are different, there
isn't any two of us the same,
We'll all react to different situations, but I guess
that's just the nature of the game,
But we shouldn't let our differences divide us,
or ever try to gain the upper hand,
Just be thankful for all that we've been given, and
let our praise be heard throughout this land.

It's only natural that we stick to our opinions, and
there may never be a meeting of our minds,
But let us concentrate on what we have in common,
for our God should be the tie that ever binds.
It's true our skins may be a different colour, and it
may well be we speak with different voice.
But a heart is still a heart in every language, And it's
in that heart that we must make our choice.

Instead of separating into factions, that really have no relevance at all,
We should proudly stand beneath our Saviours banner,
so all the world can see us standing tall.
Some of us may run towards the battle, while
others may well feel that they should hide.
But when it comes to having trust in Jesus, it's you
and only you that can decide...Amen.

BATTLES

With that day that you were dreading fast approaching,
when the fears you held become reality,
When you feel the battle's far too tough to
handle, Jesus says just hand it all to me.
When you feel the odds are strongly stacked against you,
when the strength you needs impossible to find,
When the enemy are threatening to surround you,
that's when Jesus says this battle's really mine.

The Lord's aware of how much we can handle,
and we can lean upon Him as our staff,
He'll bear our weight when we should ever need
Him, and He's there to intervene on our behalf,
If the turbulence you face is overbearing, and you
can't decide if you should sink or swim,
He's told us He won't leave us or forsake us,
let go and pass the burden unto Him,

I have lost count of the times He's fought my battles, and
He's brought me through them time and time again,
He took my place when I was faced with danger, He
took the blows and the gladly bore the pain.
While He dwells within my heart I am protected,
I can conquer every enemy I face,
But I only made it through each confrontation, knowing
Jesus Christ was there to take my place...Amen.

GRACE

A child came home from school one day, confusion on his face,
And innocently asked his mum, just what is meant by Grace.
The mother took him in her arms, as she began to cry,
Although I can't explain it all, I'll do my best to try.

Grace is never judging, and Grace is being kind.
Grace is not revengeful, and Grace is never blind.
Grace is having patience for that something that you've longed,
Grace is showing forgiveness, whenever you've been wronged.

Grace is holding unto Faith, no matter what life brings,
It's knowing there is goodness found, in every single thing.
Grace is putting trust in God, to bring you through the fight,
Grace is having confidence to know He'll put things right.

The child's grin just grew broader, with every word she said,
Thanks for explaining Mummy, for just last night I prayed,
And I thanked the Lord with all my heart,
for His love that sets me free,
And I know He heard, because I felt, His
Grace surrounding me....Amen.

SORRY

Sorry seems to be the word I use most in my prayers,
To the one who's done so much for me, and the one who truly cares.
Yet I know He always listens, when I ask wholeheartedly,
So Lord I ask you once again, please don't give up on me.

I've let you down a million times, with every passing day,
And every time we correspond, I'm sorry's all I say.
I don't intend in hurting you, so listen to my plea,
I need you Lord, I know I do, so don't give up on me.

I know I must frustrate you Lord, unworthy as I am,
You gave your Son because of me as a sacrificial lamb.
And every gift you've given me, I accepted selfishly,
But please forgive my weakness Lord, and don't give up on me.

If you should throw me to the wolves, I really can't complain,
For the promises I've broken Lord, time and time again,
But I trust you won't desert me Lord, I ask abide with me,
For life would be unbearable, if you give up on me....Amen.

ADDICTION

Did that alcohol you drank last night, make your worries melt away?
Or simply offer some escape, til you woke up today.
And how about those friends you made,
when you bought them all a round?
Yet this morning when you need a friend, their nowhere to be found.

Maybe if you pop those pills, you bought the night before,
Perhaps they'll offer some relief, for the problem that's in store.
But your old enough to realise, for you've tried them in the past,
Their escape is far from permanent, their effects will never last.

It's time to think outside the box, for you need a better plan,
There's only heartaches to be found, in a bottle or a can.
And drugs are no solution or the answer that you crave,
They only lead to misery and perhaps an early grave.

Jesus offers guidance, when the future's looking grim,
Never underestimate how much you mean to Him.
He's holding out His hand to you, He sees the tears you cry,
If you've exhausted all the rest. give the Lord a try....Amen.

5

RELATIONSHIP

I'm aware that non-believers hold me up to scrutiny,
And make their final judgement based on what they see in me.
But yet I'm just a sinner, who's no better than the rest,
Without Jesus just a loser, if you put me to the test.

Never try to judge the Lord, by what I say or do,
Your sure to find some faults in me, and I expect you to.
For only one was perfect, and His light will never dim,
Look beyond the faults in me, and focus just on Him

For it wasn't I who gave my life to take your sin away,
And it isn't I you'll answer to, when comes your judgement day.
Letting go of comparisons, is the best thing you can do,
For your relationship with Jesus, is just between you two...Amen.

SATAN

Satan tears the dreams we have asunder, his
lies are like a rapier to our heart,
The lives that took us so long in the building, in
an instant he can tear them all apart.
He needs your soul to keep Hells fires burning,
he'll twist the truth in every way he can,
He'll spin a web from which there's no escaping,
until he owns the heart of every man.

He always seems to prey upon our weakness, and
targets those who he regards a threat.
I spare a thought for all of those he's captured,
for eternity's a long time to regret.
But my defence is in the name of Jesus, His
very name alone will be my shield,
And while I know that I have His protection,
Satan's lies can never make me yield.

Although he comes to me in many guises, and
there may be times he takes me by surprise,
But when I'm weak I call on my Redeemer, and He's
there to help me see though his disguise.
A shield of Grace the Lord has placed around
me, so I am not alone to face my fate,
So in spite of all that Satan has to offer, it's a shield
that he will never penetrate...Amen.

HE LEADS

I have stood aloft the very highest mountain, and
felt the tears of joy run down my face,
Yet I've also felt the deepest darkest anger, wishing
there was someone else to take my place.
I have travelled through the spectrum of emotions,
from joy to pain and everything between,
I've took pleasure in the life that I've been given, yet
I've witnessed things I wish I'd never seen.

There's been times I've felt the comfort of the sunshine,
yet also times I've cursed the Winter cold,
There's been times for looking back and reminiscing,
more so now that I am growing old.
But all throughout this life that I've been given, in
every journey made both near and far,
I know the Lord has always been beside me,
even in my very darkest hour.

It's this that lifts my spirit's when deflated, for I
know no matter how bad things may feel,
As long as I retain my Faith in Jesus, tomorrow
all the scars will start to heal.
Every day's a bright and new beginning, another
chance to wipe the blackboard clean,
For I know that when the Lord decides to take me, He will
lead me to those pastures new and green...Amen.

POLITICS

While we place our trust in so-called politicians,
we might as well be clutching unto straws,
For democracy goes flying out the window, when
they introduce their own self-centred laws,
They will close ranks for the fear of being discovered,
so their underhanded dealings go unseen.
They make promises they don't intend on keeping,
that's the way it is and way it's always been.

Perhaps I need to be more understanding, but
believe me I have done my best to try,
But tell me what they've done to tackle problems,
or how many hungry children have to die?
I thank the Lord there is a greater power, the
only one in whom I place my trust,
The Eternal God who's reign will last forever,
while every other empire turns to dust.

I believe that we must turn to Him in trouble, in
this world where so much tragedy appears,
For I believe the politicians do not listen, but
when we speak to God He always hears.
We only seem to hear from those in power,
whenever an election's drawing near,
But God is there and listens to our prayers, three
hundred, and sixty-five days every year

So in the Lord I'll place my trust forever, so I
ask you politicians please take note,
He's the only one who's kept His every promise,
and the only one that's worthy of my vote.
So until it comes my time to leave this body, let
the balances of power swing to and fro,
I have placed my X beside the name of Jesus, that's
the only place I know that it should go....Amen.

IF ONLY

If only there was more that I could offer, If only
there was more that I could give,
But everything I have is insufficient, for the one
who gave His life that I might live.
They could take away my every source of comfort,
and I wouldn't be regretful at the loss,
For this very life I have I owe to Jesus, when He
gladly took my place upon that cross.

And even when He died it wasn't finished, for
He rose again and left me with a plea,
That if I choose to trust in you Lord Jesus, You'll
return when you've prepared a place for me.
And yet I look around and see indifference, with
selfishness and ignorance on show,
If only there was some way to convince them, of
the magnitude of just how much they owe.

But the debt was paid and seems to be forgotten, The
blood He shed has wiped the blackboard clean,
He paid the price for all of our transgressions,
and we carry on as if it were unseen.
But someday we must stand before His Father,
and all too soon we'll come to realise,
That all of us have made a contribution, to what
took place that day before our eyes....Amen.

CALL

It may well be you think that you are powerless,
there's nothing you can do to end your strife,
But it only takes a drop or two of water, to make
that dormant seed spring into life.
Maybe you just lack the motivation, or believe
that things can never be the same,
But there's a loving pair of hands out there to help
you, and all you have to do is call His name.

If it feels like you're forever treading water, but
never really seem to move along.
Rooted to the spot you've been allotted, yet
feeling that it's not where you belong.
Maybe once you rose to meet each challenge, but
the wind has all been taken from your sails,
Maybe then it's time to come to Jesus, and
discover He has love that never fails.

If you feel that you've examined all your options, I
wonder have you gave the Lord a glance,
Even if you've lived your life a sinner, He's
always there to give a second chance.
When you feel that life has thrown you in the gutter,
there's just the one direction you can go,
Ask the Lord and He'll provide the water, and then
that dormant seed can start to grow.....Amen.

REVIVAL

Lives are being turned around, like they've never been before,
As Revival starts to take a hold, each day we witness more.
So let's all join together, to pray it doesn't cease,
Young and old, rich and poor, let the numbers please increase,

It's good the Lord is winning hearts, and the battle's being won,
On every front He's taking ground, Praise be to the Son.
Churches start to fill again, and Heaven celebrates,
Endless queues begin to form, outside of Heavens gates.

There's blessings in abundance, for those who serve the Lord,
There's harmony, when we agree, and live in one accord.
It may have took a little while, but the message's getting through,
Of how much He loves His children, and the wonders He can do.

Defeat can turn to victory, and a grimace to a smile,
A simple prayer is all it takes, to make a life worthwhile.
The Lord is coming back again, the battles almost won,
His children are preparing, for the Glory that's to come....Amen.

ALL FOR FREE

It's not that He demands from us a ransom,
in fact there isn't anything to pay,
To the one who gave His only Son at Calvary, and
by who's blood our sins are washed away.
There's nothing that should cause us any worry,
and nothing detrimental causing pain,
He only asks we give our hearts to Jesus, so
He can help us be reborn again.

There isn't any sacrifice demanded, in spite of
all the things you may have heard,
Jesus paid the debt that was outstanding, He
gave His life for you because He cared.
You may well see a change in how your thinking,
but that's because the Lord has set you free,
And when you have the Holy Ghost to guide
you, those changes all occur so naturally.

So consider very carefully His offer, and then
make up your mind what you must do,
For we may escape our judgement while we're living,
but there's a higher power that we must answer to.
The Lord above is waiting for your answer, and
it's only you my friend that can decide,
For very soon we'll see the Lord returning, and then
there will be no place left to hide...Amen.

FOR JOHN.

The journey that I'm taking is a long one, but
I've no idea how long the trip will last,
I only know I need the help of Jesus, and His
forgiveness for the sin of all my past.
The problems that I'm facing may be many, and I
know there's some impossible to mend.
But all I have to do is ask forgiveness, so there's
a better future waiting at the end.

No-one is beyond the love of Jesus, no matter
what has happened in the past,
His open arms, a sign that you are welcome,
and all you really have to do is ask.
The sin I have cannot prevent Him caring,
for after all it was for sin He died,
And I know He'll listen when I choose to call Him,
For He knows of every tear I've ever cried.

Every day's a gift sent down from Heaven, and
none of us can really know for sure,
Yet it doesn't really matter just how many, if
Jesus knows the heart we have is pure.
And even in our very darkest moments, when
all around is growing very dim,
As long as we have breath within our bodies,
It's not too late to give our lives to Him.

And what reward we'll see if that should happen,
can a prayer make it as easy as it seems,
And we can meet again with friends and family, in
a place beyond the wildest of our dreams.
We only have to place our Faith in Jesus, who's
light is so much brighter than the Sun,
And when the final breath has left our body, we'll
see how easily death is overcome...Amen.

GIANTS

It feels like we're forever battling giants, and
they represent the sum of all our fears,
Yet every time we knock one down before
us, just to find another one appears.
But remember that the Bible clearly tells us,
and I believe that every word is true,
The greatest power on Earth can ever equal, the
power that Jesus Christ has placed in you.

Maybe it's the bully in the playground, or the
coldness in a heart that never warms,
Maybe just the thought of isolation, for giants
come in many different forms.
Maybe it's the thought of growing older, or the
King who rules his kingdom out of fear,
Just remember God is so much bigger, and
know that He is ever standing near.

If only we possessed the Faith of David,
every time we take to battlefield,
And recognise we have the Lords protection, our
Faith alone would never let us yield.
Do you really think that God would see us suffer,
and let us face those giants all alone?
If He sent His only Son to die at Calvary, then
He'd never let us fight them on our own.

So the next time you are staring at a giant,
remember how a boy with just a sling,
Overcame and killed a mighty giant, and
eventually that boy became a King.
Each and every day we'll face a giant, Yet
still they never seem to realize
That the God we serve provides us with the armour,
to bring the tallest giant down to size....Amen.

CHRISTMAS

The Christmas tree stands proudly in the corner,
with multi-coloured lights on every limb,
But do we celebrate the birth of Jesus, or is it
just at Christmas we remember Him?
The message of the season should be joyous,
for giving thanks for all that we enjoy,
But it's not about St Nicholas or his reindeer,
but about the birth of Mary's little boy.

Is the message lost in all the wrapping paper, do
we never give our Saviour any thought,
Do we forget the cross and how He bled at Calvary,
or remember how our liberty was bought.
See the candles flicker by the fireside, look
at all those presents by the bed,
See the Holly with it's crimson berries, that
reminds me of the blood that Jesus shed.

But above all don't forget to teach the children,
before they bring their presents out to play,
That it's all because we've gained the love of Jesus,
we come to celebrate this Christmas day.
For all too soon they'll reach the same conclusion,
that Santa and his grotto was a myth,
The reality is all because of Jesus, that we
celebrate December twenty-fifth.

So when the Christmas tree's been decorated,
and all the family gathers to applaud,
Take a moment to remember Jesus, and say a
prayer to give your thanks to God.
Then maybe if you glance out of the window, you
may well see the snow fall all around,
Then thank the Lord for sending us Salvation, in the
form of the little boy that He sent down....Amen.

THE TUNNEL

There's a light at the end of the tunnel, that leads to a glorious day,
The trouble is you'll never find it, if your facing the opposite way.
If you're stumbling around in the darkness,
that exit will never be found,
But there's guidance out there when you need
it, all you have to do's turn around.

If it feels like you're trapped in a bubble, or
maybe you're caught in a web,
Drowning in seas full of sorrow, in a land where the seas never ebb.
If the burdens you carry are heavy, your brought
down by the weight of your task,
There's a hand reaching out to relieve you,
He is waiting whenever you ask.

If you feel that the hole's getting deeper, with
the walls of your room closing in,
If your frantically looking solutions, but not
certain where you should begin.
When the swamp that's your life's overwhelming,
and you feel like your gasping for air,
Carry your worries to Jesus, and I'm certain that He will be there.

The Lord knows of all your dilemmas, and
the suffering your going through,
He suffered the torture of Calvary, so
remember that He's felt them too.
Just put your trust in the Saviour, He's
aware of the hardships you face,
He'll ensure that the worries you carry, are removed
by the power of His Grace.....Amen.

SECRETS

Oh Lord you know the truth of all I'm saying, for
you know the deepest secrets of my heart,
You have helped with every storm I've had to conquer,
for you were always there to take my part.
But you'll also know what causes me most anguish,
so there isn't any reason I must tell.
It's the prayer I sent for all my friends and family, that
they might come to know you Lord as well.

You know that when I leave this Earthly body,
it really will not cause me any pain,
But the hardest load that I am made to carry, is the
thought that I won't see them all again.
If only there was some way to convince them,
that they are all included in your plan,
That would make me cast away my worries, and
leave this world a more contented man.

But I will place my trust in you Lord Jesus, to
take away the scales from every eye,
So one day I will see them in your Kingdom,
where we'll be re-united when we die.
My hopes are resting in the blood of Jesus, as I look
towards the cross where He was nailed.
For I know that you will gather all your children, and be
successful Lord where I've so often failed...Amen.

GALILEE

They were frightened by the storm that broke around
them, but what a marvellous sight they got to see,
When the hand of Jesus calmed the stormy waters
as He walked upon the Sea of Galilee,
And suddenly the fear in them subsided, as
they realised their Master was at hand,
How could any mortal come to doubt Him, when
the elements bow down to His command.

And then there came the wedding down at Canaan,
where we saw Him turn the water into wine,
The miracle of barley loaves and fishes that
fed the multitude who stood in line.
There was the way He chose to walk among the lepers,
and the way he cured the sick man by the lake,
Restoring sight and bringing light to darkness,
and then exposing Satan as a fake.

The sermon that He gave upon the Mountain, and
the way that He rose Lazarus from the grave.
The crucifixion, then the resurrection, His
sacrifice the only way to save.
For the blood He shed has still retained its
power, to carry every sinners sin away,
And so much evil's been transformed to goodness, so
He's still performing miracles to-day...Amen.

LOST SUNDAYS

What happened to those Sundays, the ones that used to please,
Their now completely different, just like chalk and cheese.
The children had their weekly wash, in a tin bath by the fire,
Father dried us with a towel, and Mum with her hair-dryer.

The smell of breakfast cooking, brought water to our lips.
But first we had to make our beds, with brand new pillow slips.
Then we sat around the table, as ten o'clock drew near,
And sang "why are we waiting", til our breakfast did appear.

We were never really angry, but did our best to understand,
When we were woken in the morning by a Salvation Army band,
Dad would read the papers, while Mum was getting dressed,
And all of us set off for church, attired in our Sunday best.

Sunday's then were special, in many different ways,
A day for giving thanks to God, and sending Him our praise.
It was the day we set aside for God, the day we gave to Him,
And not for simply playing golf, or going to the gym....Amen.

NATIVITY

One star outshone all others, in Bethlehem that night,
As it hovered in the evening sky, to bathe the world in light.
It signalled a new beginning, to a world so ripped and torn,
As it paused above a stable, where a baby boy was born.

For this tiny little bundle, who lay in a manger curled,
Beneath that hay, Would grow someday, as the Saviour of the world.
And the news went round so quickly, and
the shepherds left their herds,
To come and pay their homage, with excitement in their words.

Hope had been reborn again, in the form of just a child,
But a child sent down from Heaven, with a temperament so mild.
And as Mary looked upon her babe, the
tears streamed down her face,
Bewildered, but yet thankful, for that miracle taking place.

And Jesus slumbered peacefully, on that night so dark and still,
The Son of Man who came to Earth, to fulfil His Fathers will.
A lamb into a lion's den, a penetrating light.
And hope was born along with Him, on
that first Christmas night....Amen.

LESSONS

I thought my lessons over, when my school-days all had past,
No more counting minutes for the finish of the class.
A brave new world awaited me, at least that's what I said,
But school had not prepared me for the things that lay ahead.

For I was young and foolish then, and thought I knew it all,
But there were hurdles just ahead, and I would trip and fall.
I never really understood, that life was very short,
And we must come to terms with death, for that was never taught.

But as the years went rolling by, my wrinkles soon appeared,
And each day brought me closer, to the thing that I most feared.
But then I heard of Jesus, and how Forgiveness can be won,
How eternal life was purchased, when a Father gave His Son.

So I offered up the sinners prayer, and He took me as His own,
I would have done it years ago, if only I had known.
But still the Lord accepted me, and every day I pray,
School has gone but still I'm learning new things every day....Amen.

SILENCE

Is it better to be silent, and preserve the harmony,
Than to raise our voice in protest, when we strongly disagree.
Is it proper just ignoring, when we see that something's wrong,
Does life become much easier, if we just play along.

Should we close our eyes to evil and pretend that it's not there.
Be indifferent to suffering, or demonstrate we care.
If we maintain our silence, the perpetrator gets the vote,
Should we deny we even saw it, so as not to rock the boat.

In every situation there's a way we should behave,
Jesus gave directions, in the lessons that He gave.
There are times we must be silent, and
there's times we need to speak,
With His presence there to guide us, seven days in every week.

He provides the strength when needed,
when the road has made us tired,
We should give our love to others, yet take a stand when its required,
We must reach the highest standards, and
never compromise our Faith,
Showing bravery in adversity, knowing He will keep us safe...Amen.

RELATIONSHIPS

Relationships can fracture, and friendships fall apart,
One day we admire someone, the next a change of heart.
Disagreements surface and arguments pursue,
Until we find that friend we had, is not the one we knew.

Like clouds that drift across the sky, forever changing shape,
Submission then becomes the bars, preventing our escape.
Friends we once relied upon, then start to let us down,
And when we're needing their support, we find their not around.

If this all sounds familiar, and you have saw this too,
There's just the one piece of advice, that I can offer you.
There's one who won't desert you, He's the friend that I have found,
From the moment of conception, until they lay me in the ground.

He's there when you should need Him, considerate and true,
He'll lift you spirits, raise you up, like no-one else can do.
He's loving and forgiving, and never seeks to blame,
He gave His life to show His love, and Jesus is His name....Amen.

WORTHLESS

We tend to look on useless things, then simply throw away,
To us they've lost their value, and that's always been the way.
Why waste time and effort, in something we don't need?
So we just move on to better things, that satisfy our greed.

But what if Jesus felt the same, when He looked down on us?
As something to be thrown away, and hardly worth the fuss.
Why should He invest His time, in what has caused Him strife,
One who holds no value, yet for whom He gave His life.

So I guess there must be value, in the soul of every man,
Maybe we can't see it, and only Jesus can,
Otherwise He'd just give up, and do the very same,
Confine us to the garbage, with only us to blame.

But thankfully that's not the case, to Him we mean much more,
He thinks so very much of us, as well worth dying for.
If you ask yourself why anyone would give their life for me,
It's 'cause Jesus looks on worthless things
and sees them differently....Amen.

THE STORY

The only book that ever brings me comfort, is
the one that tells of Jesus Christ my King,
I read about a baby born of Mary, and how
the life He led changed everything.
How disciples were created out of fishermen, and
how He healed the leper with His hand,
How He always used to speak with us in parables,
in a language all of us can understand.

He spoke about the reason for His coming,
to carry off the sins of every man,
That He would pay the bill that was outstanding,
and He would be the sacrificial lamb.
He inspired us to always love our neighbours, and
gave us words that taught us how to pray,
He was crucified between two common criminals,
but rose again and still lives to this day.

So I believe the story's not yet finished, there's
still another chapter to be read,
And I believe some day I'll get to read it, when
all the world believes me to be dead,
For I will rise the way the good Lord promised,
and I will get to see Him on His throne,
And there I'll give my praise among the Angels,
whenever He decides to call me home...Amen.

TOO LATE

I never made the time to get to know you, there
was always something else got in the way,
And now I find I'm seated in this hallway, for this
has now become my judgement day.
I realise I used up all my chances, such sheer
regret I'm feeling deep inside
For I know that soon that door is going to open,
and Heavens Court is on the other side.

I know I never asked the Lords forgiveness, and
therefore I still carry all my crime,
But the strains of how I managed my existence,
meant it seemed I never really had the time.
Yet I feel that I am clawing for excuses, when
in truth the fault was really only mine,
If I had only asked to be forgiven, everything
would then have worked out fine.

I see now how my life was truly wasted, as I
listen for the opening of that door,
I realise I've given very little, when I know I
could have given so much more.
If only I had listened as He called me, but I
guess that I was just too blind to see,
If only I had gave my life to Jesus, for after all He gave His life for me.

I should have listened carefully to His message,
and adhered to every word He ever said,
And I only hope you'll listen to my story, to avoid
the same mistakes that I have made,
Open up your heart and let Him enter, for it's
then that you can know your truly saved,
If only I had gained the love of Jesus, instead of
all the other things I craved...Amen.

DISTRACTED

Distractions cloud our visions, and make it difficult to see,
But how about when you're alone, with only thoughts for company?
In those solitary moments, when the noise has fizzled out,
Do you ever come to ask yourself, what life is all about?

Do you ever search for purpose, or ask why you are here?
Do you use the opportunity, when no-one else is near?
Are you trying hard to find yourself, or the one you're meant to be?
Have you reached the summit of your life, or is there more to see?

How will friends remember you, when you are not around?
When all that's left to remind them, is a headstone in the ground.
Surely then you understand, that you are worth much more,
There has to be a better plan, as to what your living for.

The answer lies in Jesus, if you really think it through,
He sacrificed His life, so He must have a plan for you,
There's direction if you ask Him, He's waiting for your call,
For every life is precious, and He's a purpose for us all...Amen.

THE MEMORY

Calvary's vision haunts me, and I guess it always will,
Such cruelty was put on show, upon that murderous hill.
The worst in men had surfaced, by the actions that they took,
As the bloodshed and the suffering, made it difficult to look.

The cross, the spear, that crown of thorns, emblazoned on my mind,
A tragedy so terrible, impossible to find.
But the grief I feel evaporates, and turns to joy instead,
When I focus my attention, on that third day just ahead.

For the Son of Man is still alive, and living to this day,
Calvary so regrettable, yet there was no other way.
The sins of Man were many, So an innocent had to die,
But it wasn't nails that held Him there, but the sin of you and I.

I won't forget what happened, to Jesus Christ the Son,
We might have lost a battle, but the war was not yet won.
For the tomb is my reminder, when that stone was rolled away,
That the Son of God's immortal, and is still alive this day...Amen.

THE MESSAGE

Keep your eyes on Jesus, and every word He said,
His wisdom's there for all to read, distinctly marked in red.
For truth's the key, to set us free, from the chains that have us bound,
And nowhere in this world of ours, can so much truth be found.

Keep your eyes on Jesus, and the message that He brings,
Son of God, Emmanuel, Almighty King of Kings.
The light of hope eternal, in a world that's growing dim,
The only route to Heaven, when we place our trust in him.

Keep your eyes on Jesus, and the promise that he gave,
There's mercy for the sinner, and there's freedom for the slave.
And only by the blood He shed, can sin be swept away,
Call Him and He'll answer, He's the life, the truth, the way.

Keep your eyes on Jesus, set all other thoughts aside,
For evil's days are numbered and He's coming for His bride.
Desperation threatens, and times are growing grim,
But there's nothing left, that we should fear, when
we keep our eyes on Him....Amen.

YOU CAME

You came to Earth as mortal, with all the pain that brings,
When you could have come in splendour, everlasting King of Kings.
Your home became the highway, not the mansion you deserve,
You tackled Satan in his lair, when no-one had the nerve.

You walked among your people, and by
your love you gained their trust,
You confronted all your enemies, When you
could have and scattered them like dust.
You calmed the seas for fishermen, and made the blind to see,
You bled and died at Calvary, to save the likes of me.

To me, the joy of knowing you, is worth much more that gold,
That story of how you lived your life, the greatest ever told.
Yet the story doesn't end there, there's a chapter still to come,
For your coming back to lead us, to the
place your coming from.....Amen.

SENT

You said your Father sent you, to save the likes of me,
And every word you uttered I believed explicitly.
You said that I could be with you, if I called upon your name,
That the gift of life is found in you, and we only have to claim.

And that is why I gave my heart and entrusted it to you,
For after all you did for me, it's the least that I could do.
You died to take my sin away, before I knew your name,
And after all the wrong I do, your love remains the same.

I'm happy that I found you Lord, you made my life complete,
And all the cares that life throws down, I lay them at your feet.
I thank the day I came to you, and you took me for your own,
You placed a seed within my heart, and how that seed has grown.

For the cornerstone is missing, without Jesus by your side,
It's like trying to host a wedding, when there isn't any bride.
We need Him there beside us, He's the key that fits the lock,
He's the guardian of His children, and the
Shepherd of the flock....Amen.

BLESSINGS

The Blessings Heaven pours on us, are gifts sent from afar,
But it's how we choose to use them, that makes us who we are.
We should use them for His Glory, as they come down from above,
And He'll furnish all we'll ever need, as a token of His love.

Solomon's gift was wisdom, and Abraham's a son.
Noah's was a warning, just before the floods begun.
Jacob had his ladder, and Joseph had his robe,
Samson his amazing strength, with patience gave to Job.

Ruth was given Boaz, and David had the psalms,
Moses granted leadership, that led to the Promised Land.
Paul became a writer, the best this World has seen,
And Daniel given insight to interpret any dream.

Nothings unachievable, there's nothing in the rules,
If Jesus has a task for you, He'll give you all the tools,
If you think your time has been and gone, the Sun has not yet set,
The Lord above has plans for you and He's not finished yet....Amen.

TRUST

There isn't any middle-ground, or space for compromise,
You either trust in Jesus Christ, or fall for Satan's lies.
You can never sit upon the fence, or try to hedge your bets,
You can seek forgiveness from the Lord, or live with your regrets.

You can walk towards the light He shines, or stay hidden in the dark,
You can follow Him, or take the route that falls short of the mark.
You can wallow in the lies and filth, and believe you've everything,
Or drown in all the truth and joy that only He can bring.

You can always take the easy route, and believe all Satan says,
But have you thought what's coming next,
you can't have it both ways.
Perhaps you think you've lots of time, to make things right with God,
But that belief makes Heaven weep, and all in Hell applaud.

Time is running out my friend, there's not long left to choose,
The candles getting shorter, there's no time left on the fuse,
Decision time is looming, there's no time to hang around,
For one day soon all Earth will get to hear
that trumpet sound.....Amen.

HE CARES

Are we really ever outside of His care,
Is there any way of knowing He is there.
Will the love He holds be shown, will He make His presence known,
Will there be a sweet aroma in the air.

Will He listen should I offer up my plea,
And will I know that He's accepted me.
Will the sin I own depart, Will He repair my broken heart.
Will He take away these chains to set me free.

For I've been told, that He'll accept me as I am,
I've been told that He will take me by the arm.
That I should come to Him today, and that He turns no-one away,
So this storm that's been my life, can be made calm.

Then I wonder just how far we have to fall,
Before we decide to answer Jesus' call.
Just how far we have to sink, before He draws us from the brink,
And realise that Jesus loves us all....Amen.

A GLIMPSE

If we could see a little piece of Heaven, just
a glimpse before our time is due,
And then a sight of the other place on offer,
thereby allowing us to compare the two.
What a different World we would be seeing,
knowing what is lying just ahead,
Gone would be the evil so apparent, and we
might witness Godliness instead.

If we could dwell forever with the Angels, instead
of sulphur stinging both our eyes,
If we could just avoid that fiery furnace, but
worship God with Heaven as our prize,
Maybe Heavens gates could be left open, so all
of us could have safe passage through,
Then the gates of Hell forever would be fastened, If
we love the Lord then this can all come true.

For the dream that I'm describing can all happen,
if we start to see the changes taking place,
For the Sins of Men have been already purchased, the
bill was settled due to God's amazing Grace.
We only need to have the motivation, and the
reward is waiting for us at the end,
And if we take the hand that Jesus offers,
eventually this World can start to mend.

For as long as we have got the Lords protection,
Satan cannot tempt us any more,
He will only hear the cries of celebration,
whenever we arrive at Heavens shore.
As long as we're prepared to follow Jesus, then
the chances we don't make it will be slim,
We can get to wear the crown that He has offered, but all
the Glory and the Honour rests with Him....Amen.

THE WORD

We cannot change the word of God, it's not a game we play,
If it was sin two thousand years ago, then it's still a sin today.
There are those who try to alter, how we determine crime,
But the law that God has given us, withstands the test of time,

So many rules are being changed, to get us off the hook,
By those who claim to serve the Lord, yet contradict His book,
Things are made acceptable, we once looked upon with scorn,
A million miles and growing, from what the truth is based upon.

But when we stand in judgement, we won't face the laws of Men,
Instead we'll face our maker, and how will we feel then?
Did we follow as He asked us, did we obey all His commands?
Or did we grab the loopholes, that were placed into our hands?

We were given Ten Commandments, did we live our lives by these,
Or try to move the goalposts, to live exactly as we please.
I know I make some errors, but I try to do my best,
Yet if honesty is spoken, I'm as guilty as the rest...Amen.

THE ARK

They ran towards the mountains, as the rain came pouring down,
Hoping to find shelter, when they reached the higher ground.
But the waters just kept rising, and by now had reached their knees,
All because they'd turned their backs towards
the God they used to please.

Mothers cradled babies to protect them from the rain,
Yet fell victim to that torrent, that the World won't see again,
For a mountain cannot save us, when God's anger starts to pour,
And He had watched in desperation, until He could watch no more.

They had watched as Noah's family, started building that great ark,
They had laughed in pure amusement,
until the sky was growing dark.
It was only then they realised, the cost for all their sin,
That with Noah safely in the ark, the rain could now begin.

And the waters kept on rising, and the ark began to rise,
And the evil was all banished, one could tell it from their cries.
And when the ark had come to settle, only eight remained,
But a Rainbow formed in Heaven, as God's
Kingdom was regained....Amen.

RICHES

Money has it's purpose, who am I to disagree,
Yet the best that life can offer us, is still completely free.
There's so many things of beauty, that money can't supply,
And all of these, and so much more, money just can't buy.

The beauty of a Sunset, when the Moon is on the rise,
The satisfaction that we feel, as our child collects their prize.
A new born baby sleeping, tiny fingers pink and curled,
Can't be exchanged for all the gold and silver in the world.

The golden streams of daybreak, as we open up our eyes,
The clouds that change their patterns, as they drift across the skies,
The pure refreshing water, that we draw from crystal stream,
A loving hand caressing us, as we're drifting off to dream.

Growing old together, and the health that we enjoy,
Watching children growing into manhood from a boy.
These are gifts from Heaven, priceless and yet free,
And I thank my God for all His Grace, in giving them to me...Amen.

ENLIGHTENED

There were portions of the Bible, I found hard to understand,
So I went in search of someone, who could lend a helping hand,
I bought a little notebook and I wrote my questions out.
Then a list of people who could help remove all trace of doubt.

I spoke to all my pastors, and they offered where they could,
I engaged with friends and family, and anyone who would.
There were differing opinions, as to what some verses meant,
But everyone still gave their best no matter where I went.

But then a notion surfaced, that I'd missed along the way,
There was one who holds the answers, and He listens when I pray.
If I ask Him for enlightenment, He'll clarify it all,
He'll answer all my queries, both the big ones and the small.

So I threw away my notebook, and that list of names as well,
I knew God had the answers and I knew that He would tell.
So there were explanations given and confusion reigns no more,
It was then I came to realise, I should have
asked the Lord before....Amen.

FOR

For every word of thanks that went unspoken,
For every promise made, that then was broken.
For my multitude of sin, for every doubt I let creep in,
I apologise, though words are just a token.

For the many times I must have let you down,
For your tears, that formed a river on the ground.
For these eyes that failed to see, all that you required of me,
Though you freed me from the chains that had me bound.

For the Blessings that you give me through your Grace,
For the Son who went to Calvary in my place.
For the gift of each new day, for the debt I can't repay,
For the selfishness of all the Human Race.

For the love you send that always brings me through,
Though I know the pain my sin is causing you.
When tomorrow comes along, Keep me safe from doing wrong,
And just help me Lord to make it up to you....Amen.

HEAVENS SWEET MUSIC

I stood alone at Heavens Gates, and heard the Angels sing,
There was never such a sweeter sound,
than the praises that they'd bring.
The music that accompanied them, sent shivers down my spine,
A sound beyond description, so impossible to define.

With ears so unacquainted to such enchanting melody,
As voices joined with violins, making perfect harmony.
Nothing else I've ever felt, could equal that desire,
That filled my very heart and soul, as I listened to that choir.

But then an interruption, as it came my time to rise,
My alarm gave out it's warning, and I opened up my eyes.
I was brought back to reality, what I'd seen and heard were dreams,
For dawn had torn my visions, and then ripped them at the seams.

But I know deep in this heart of mine, whenever time is due,
Someday what I dreamt last night, is going to come true.
I'll get to hear those sounds again, but sweeter than before,
When I stand alone at Heavens Gates, and
alarms will ring no more.....Amen.

CHINA

Oh China if your listening, let the persecution stop,
Satan's making slaves of you, he's caught you in his trap.
When you subdue the word of God, that's a sin He can't forget,
Yet you stigmatise your people, when they offer you no threat.

When you target all their churches, is it giving you a thrill?
Your trying to break you people, when you know you never will.
The hand of God is mighty, He has seen it all before,
He's defeated many armies, when His anger starts to pour.

I remember Saul of Tarsus, and that Damascus Road,
And how he did the same as you, His story's widely told.
But then there came conversion, when his eyes were made to see,
If only you could be like him, and set your people free.

They only yearn to worship, with neither fear nor threat,
But still we see such tragedies, this world cannot forget.
By silencing your Christians, what have you to gain?
For there'll come a day, not long from now,
when you must all explain...Amen.

GEORGE

No-one saw the pain she had to carry, and no-
one thought to ask her how she felt,
The only hope that she had left to cling to, was
in her prayers, as by her bed she knelt.
The family that she raised were distant memories,
for all of them had flown and left the nest,
Maybe just a card or two at Christmas, a meagre
'thank you' after giving them her best.

She was thankful for the Husband she had chosen, for
without him she would have never made it by,
How he managed to escape in situations, for he
still had that boyish twinkle in his eye.
But all that now remained were golden memories,
for yesterday, tomorrow, and today,
Yet the tears just seemed to override the laughter,
so her handkerchief was never far away.

For a week had passed since George had left for Heaven,
seven days since God had called him home,
And every passing minute seemed a lifetime,
now that she was living all alone.
But the Faith she had in Jesus was astounding, for
in her heart no anger could be found,
Just the joy at all the years they'd had together, and
the magic of the love that kept them bound.

She would miss the trips they often took together,
and the way he'd often take her by the hand,
And how he understood her deepest feelings, by
signs that no-one else could understand,
But the knowledge they'd both gave their lives to Jesus,
was the thing that carried her above the pain,
For she knew that they would re-unite in Heaven, and
there she'd get to meet with George again...Amen.

LIFE'S LESSONS

When we're taught to ride a bicycle, sometimes we might fall,
And because of inexperience, we can't expect to know it all.
But the more we persevere with it, the trick to it we'll find,
As all the grazes we picked up, are put out of our mind.

The reward we feel in riding, seems to take away the pain,
But we'll only be successful, when we get up and try again.
How our hearts are almost bursting, as we race across the ground,
Taking pleasure in the newly fangled freedom we have found.

It's all about the learning, in anything we do,
But also having confidence, when trying something new.
When I became a Christian, things kept playing on my mind,
But Jesus gave direction, just a little at a time.

It felt that I was in a race, but always finished last,
But soon I found such happiness, I hadn't in the past.
He brought me though the early days, and answered when I'd pray,
And His love was there to guide me, every step along the way...Amen.

SHINE

I do not know what lies in store, or what this day will bring,
I only know, I serve a true, and everlasting King
And I know His will must override, the wishes born of man,
So I must do all in my power to contribute to His plan.

Someone may have prayed to Him, though I was unaware,
And He may make our paths to cross, as an answer to their prayer.
So just a single action, or a word I get to speak,
May give them back the confidence, or answer that they seek.

I'll live by His commandments, it's in these I place my trust,
Just do unto others, as we would have them do to us.
For someday soon, it may well be, for we can never tell.
He'll send someone to rescue you, when you need help as well,

Offer hope to others, be that bell that chimes,
And Grace and Mercy is repaid, one hundred thousand times.
Shine a light for Jesus, in all you say and do,
And He'll ensure that when required, He'll
shine His light for you...Amen.

HOPE REBORN

My world crashed down around me, when I heard that you had died,
My hopelessness apparent, from all those tears I cried.
I tried to carry on with life, but the sadness still showed through,
For every hope and dream I held, was resting Lord in you.

I believed in all you promises, your words held me engrossed,
But how they took your life away, well, that's what hurt the most.
The pain I felt in losing you, had cut me like a knife,
For you said you were the Son of God, and that cost you your life.

But the world just kept on spinning, with neither grief nor care,
It was just as though you'd never lived, as if you were not there.
But to those who listened carefully to all you had to say,
We perished just the same as you, at Calvary that day.

But the clouds that gathered overhead, were soon to melt away,
As even we, could not foresee, what would happen that third day.
For hope was given back to us, and we rose above the pain
When we heard that death was overcome,
and Jesus walked again....Amen.

SHARING THE LOAD

When the plan all comes together, and the task has been complete,
Then comes the time we get to rest, by pulling up a seat,
But tomorrow brings it's own demands, yet another step in time,
There'll be another river we must cross, or a hill we have to climb.

If the prospect makes you weary, that another job is due,
Perhaps it's down to all that sin, that you carry round with you.
You can find your load is lightened, and you only have to ask,
No need to suffer all alone, by the burden of the task.

You've maybe reached a watershed, that's made you stop and think,
And realised there is a God, who will not watch you sink.
It may have taken quite a while, and the years just passed you by,
You might have felt conviction, but the time for action's now.

Worries are less stressful, and hardships less severe,
When you share them all with Jesus, and
you know He's standing near.
Sin He takes away from you, and the angry heart He calms,
And life becomes more bearable, when He
takes you in His arms...Amen.

JOHN 3:16

If you open up a Bible, and find the book of John,
You'll find one verse that's written there, that
the whole book's based upon.
When you've found the book in question, go to verse sixteen,
And if you care to read it, you'll see exactly what I mean.

It tells of how a Father, gave up His only Son,
And if we place our trust in Him, Eternity is won.
The words are very simple, so all can understand,
But in a nutshell still explain, how Jesus cares for Man.

Maybe time is precious and you don't have much to spare,
But still you need to understand, and this verse makes you aware.
Take some time to read it, then thank God that your alive
The words don't take that long to read, they contain just twenty-five.

JOHN 3:16 King James Version (KJV)
For God so loved the World, that He gave His only begotten Son
That whosoever believeth in Him should not perish,
But have everlasting Life...Amen.

HIS RETURN

We need your presence Jesus, or I wouldn't send this prayer,
You told us you were coming back, and I pray we're almost there,
For Man has lost the ability, of telling right from wrong,
We need now so earnestly, we've been waiting far too long.

Corruption rests with those in power, who disrespect your laws,
Satan has them in his power and holds them in his claws.
So your the only hope we have, to make the evil stop,
For it seems that all the sediment, keeps rising to the top.

These eyes that you have given me, are swollen by my tears,
This heart of mine is broken, with the passing of the years.
It's the children I feel sorry for, as their future we condemn.
And I ask myself, what kind of world, are we going to leave for them.

That's why we need you Jesus, like we've never done before,
This world is spinning out of control. and cannot take much more.
You said you were returning, and I believe it to be true,
But the time is of your choosing, so I must leave it up to you....Amen.

FANTASY

If we live our lives in fantasy, with Pixies, gnomes and elves,
Our life becomes so cloudy, we believe in them ourselves.
We may well think we're dreaming, though our eyes are open wide,
As we find we're trapped where fantasy and reality collide.

It's important to be honest, before things go too far,
So others look upon us, and judge us just for who we are,
When I told friends I'd found Jesus, some would walk away and smile,
But knowing just how much I've gained,
made losing them worthwhile.

I don't mean to offend them, to judge them or condemn,
But if they don't accept me, then it's really up to them.
Yet I'll keep praying for them, that eventually they'll see,
And someday come to realise, they can have a friend like me.

Until then I take great pleasure, in the Saviour I have found,
Along with all my other friends, who've also stuck around.
My Faith outweighs the pain I felt, in losing one or two,
But my sin has been forgiven, by that Friend I never knew.....Amen.

FROM THE ASHES

Like a phoenix from the ashes, my Saviour rose again,
He overcame the agony, and He overcame the pain.
And if ever proof was needed, He was everything He said,
It was there for all who came to look, when
He came back from the dead.

Death could never hold Him, He had so much more to say,
And if any doubt existed, it was removed on that third day.
He had put an end to doubters, and all the stories they'd contrive,
To prove that God was still in Heaven, and His Son was still alive.

As the soldiers who had guarded Him, could only look in shock,
For how could any power on Earth, remove that heavy rock.
But they didn't count on Angels, as they looked on with dismay.
For it was they who came from Heaven, and rolled that stone away.

And everyone who saw Him, dropped to their knees and cried,
For they had witnessed Calvary, and watched Him as He died.
Yet there He stood before them, with His scars, as yet unhealed,
For He really was the Son of God, and the
truth had been revealed....Amen.

THE GAMBLE

If you think that life's a mountain, and you'll never reach the top,
And our places are dependent on where the wheel will stop.
If you believe that life's determined, by the hand that we were dealt,
Or that trying to change is futile, the coldest heart will never melt,

Well I believe in something else. that life is like a flower,
That we can rise to meet the Sun, no matter where we are.
That we all possess some talent, though in varying amounts,
We may not always finish first, but it's taking part that counts,

We'll never move a mountain, that's outside the scope of Man,
But I know that we can have a friend, in the only one who can.
The one who gave His life for us, is not difficult to find,
Who began life as a carpenter, yet gave hope to all Mankind.

Who could have walked away from us, and left us with our loss,
Yet cared for every one of us, so instead He chose the cross.
So the hardest heart can be made soft, depending how we live,
For it's in our heart true value's found, when
we've only love to give....Amen.

LEADER

If we lose sight of the target, we must readdress our aim,
And if we follow Jesus, then it's more or less the same.
But He knows we're only human, and sometimes prone to stray,
But if we ask Him earnestly, He's there to point the way.

The road we walk is perilous, with handicaps and snares,
There's demons watching out for us, to trap us in their lairs.
They're lurking in the shadows, and hoping that we break,
But we should not surrender, for there's far too much at stake.

So neither look to left or right, but focus straight ahead,
Keep marching on, from dusk to dawn, exactly where your led.
For Satan cannot tempt you, or cause you any harm,
While Jesus Christ is holding you, so firmly in His palm.

Eternity is waiting, just over yonder hill,
You only need have Faith in Him, to prove you have the will.
He will lead you through the minefield,
and the worst that life can send,
He'll be with you, as a shadow, from beginning to the end...Amen.

FATHERS SECRETS

I remember Father telling me, when I was just a boy,
How we need to put some time away, for the things that we enjoy.
How, in his days he found pleasure, although the times were tough,
In setting precious time aside, for doing childish stuff.

He tried to hide his tears away, but one or two I saw,
When he told me he was fearful, yet respectful of the law,
But the one thing that he told me, that still lives with me today,
Was when he looked me in the eye, in a firm but tearful way.

He told me time was precious, a gift from God above,
And after all is said and done, you can't put a price on love.
He told me I should cherish, what the Lord has given me,
And how was I to argue, how was I to disagree?

I really miss my father, and his passing really stings,
But we made a new discovery, while we were clearing out his things
We found a Holy Bible, in a cupboard, by his bed,
And it's pages torn and crumpled, proved
how often it was read.....Amen.

THE COURTROOM

There will come a day of reckoning, of that I have no doubt,
When Heavens court's in session, to see justice handed out.
When every single one of us, must answer for our sin,
And there'll be a rude awakening, when reality kicks in.

When every misdemeanour, whether they were large or small,
Will have to be accounted for, for Jesus saw them all.
We may well fool the courts of Men, where honesty's abused.
But lives become an open book, on that day we stand accused.

With the verdict in the balance, will there be mercy shown?
Have you claimed the blood of Jesus Christ,
has He took you for His own?
For it's only when you trust the Lord, can sin be washed away,
He died to take your punishment, at Calvary that day.

And when the verdicts handed down, as someday it will be,
And even though your guilty, they decide to set you free.
Then as your standing in the dock, bow your head and pray,
And thank God for the Son He sent, who
washed your sin away.....Amen.

SIMON AND THE CRUCIFIXION

The sound was drawing closer, to where the crowd all congregates,
So I met up with the others, just beyond the City gates.
It was just outside Jerusalem, where the town and country meets,
As the heavy cross He carried, dragged along the cobbled streets.

The sounds were growing louder, so we assumed that He was near,
For those just up ahead of us, we could hear them laugh and jeer.
And then we caught a glimpse of him, with that cross across His back,
The Roman soldiers beating Him, as their whips began to crack.

His body frail and skeletal, from the blood that he had shed,
A crimson stream that followed Him, from
those thorns upon His head.
But the heavy cross He had to bear then brought Him to His knees,
While the blows kept reigning down on Him, without respite or ease.

I made my way towards Him, as He lay upon the ground,
I bore the cross then thanked Him, for that courage I had found.
For everything He'd ever said, I believed it to be true,
Yet knowing what lay in front of Him, it was
the least that I could do......Amen.

LISTEN

A wise man listens carefully, while a fool just walks away,
For how can we respect someone, when
we don't hear what they say?
So if you've heard the voice of Jesus, yet you still ignore His call,
In refusing to accept Him, that's the greatest sin of all,

Have you really got so many friends, there's no room for one more,
How come your self-sufficient, if you don't know what lies in store?
Life can throw up problems, in the blinking of an eye,
Are you really all that confident, you've enough to see you by.

I wonder who you pray too, when you are all alone,
When disappointments haunt you, and your heart sinks like a stone.
Does there never come a moment, is your life so full of bliss,
That you never ask the question, is there more to life that this?

I can't believe you live your life, and never have a doubt,
And because you do not know the Lord, you're really missing out.
If only you could make some time, to read between the lines,
You'd find your life becomes enriched, one
hundred thousand times....Amen.

PRAYER

I send my prayers daily, and I ask for quite a lot,
Some of these He grants to me, but others He does not.
But I know that in His wisdom, He always knows what's best,
So I accept His judgement, and forget about the rest.

Sometimes I'm disappointed, and I cannot tell a lie,
But He's always furnished every need, ensuring I get by.
And although I'm not successful for everything I pray,
He may accept, He may refuse, or maybe just delay.

I'm trusting of His timing, for He doesn't make mistakes,
I'll wait until He answers me, and all the time it takes.
I never feel discouraged, even when the answers No,
His decisions are what's best for me, as time will come to show,

My faith will not diminish, it's grows stronger by the day,
I'll accept it isn't possible for everything I pray.
His will must take priority, and not my selfish greed,
For as long as I have God above, I've everything I need...Amen.

THE MESSAGE

Did they think that when they nailed you to that cross,
That the message that you taught us would be lost.
They may have killed the one they sought, but
not the message that He brought,
It was too powerful to be forgot at any cost.

They failed to see and might as well be blind,
That every drop of blood you shed was for Mankind.
That as they nailed you to that tree, it was to buy our Liberty,
With a love we thought, impossible to find

How cruel was that cross you died upon,
But your message to this day, still lingers on.
No matter what they do or say, they'll never take your words away.
They will remain whenever they're all dead and gone.

Yet in that tomb they never knew what lay in store,
For they believed that you would walk the Earth no more,
Yet after all that blood and pain, you still arose and walked again.
Because the Son of Man will live for evermore....Amen.

LOST LIFE

They can call it Termination, to try and mitigate the fact,
But in the end the title, doesn't alter how we act.
They may label it a Foetus, not a Daughter or a Son,
But if we choose Abortion, it doesn't alter what's been done.

If we take away a human life, the outcome's just the same.
We cannot change the charge we face, so we must bear the blame.
So is it just an inconvenience, that made us choose that route,
Would it require we change our lifestyle, and that really didn't suit.

Did it influence our decision, that it didn't have a voice,
Where we painted in a corner, did that influence our choice.
We can have another baby, just put it off for a later day,
Does that make it more acceptable, to take it's life away.

Someday we must answer, for doing the forbidden,
If we've took away a precious life, then we can't keep that hidden.
And just like Cain killed Abel, there will be a price to pay,
And I'm glad I'm not in your shoes, when it
comes that judgement day.....Amen.

THE DOOR

If this world should end tomorrow, as I watch my last Sun set,
I could leave this Earthly body, without a glimmer of regret.
For I know my destination, now that Jesus I have found,
And once the air has left my lungs, I'll know I'm Heaven bound.

He called me and I answered, and He took me by the hand,
And all at once I understood, the workings of God's plan.
That salvation isn't promised and freedom isn't free,
But He bled and died on Calvary's cross, to purchase it for me.

It may have took a little while for me to come to see,
Yet Jesus kept on knocking, hoping I would turn the key.
And when I opened up the door, He was standing there,
As the guilt I felt in ignoring Him, became too much to bear.

But He told me He's forgiven me, and my heart began to calm,
That my sin was all forgiven and He'd accept me as I am.
Now I know what lies ahead of me, when
my days on Earth are through,
Just open up that door to Him, and you can share it too.....Amen.

THE ACT

Are we really so consistent, as the image we portray,
Or when we see someone in trouble, do we look the other way?
Do we always show our best side, for the purpose of the shot?
Are we giving the impression, we are something that we're not?

Have our friends become our audience, do we set out to impress?
Do they know we have a dark side, or would they never guess?
Would they trust us with their secrets, knowing we would never tell,
Not suspecting there's another, darker side to us as well.

Are we selective in what we're showing, just enough, but never more,
So they never see what's lurking on the other side of the door.
Then maybe we personify, all the things they long to be,
But if they scrape away the surface, I wonder what they'd see.

For when we stand in judgement, we cannot act the part,
It's not the things we did or said, but what lies in our heart.
For none of us are perfect, God will judge us by our sins,
And when the final curtain falls, eternity begins......Amen.

ANDREW

Andrew led a decent life, considerate and kind,
A better Dad or husband, you'd be doing well to find.
He got on well with everyone, like every neighbour should,
And if he could help in any way, I'm certain that he would.

But although he sometimes thought of
God, it always slipped his mind,
For Satan just kept telling him that he had lots of time.
And although, if asked, he'd give away, everything he owned,
The thought of Jesus in his life, just seemed to get postponed.

He worked hard for his children, they were the highlight of his life,
He married his childhood sweetheart and he took her for his wife.
But he fooled himself believing, there was still time to be saved,
It didn't take priority over the other things he craved.

He was only thirty-seven, when his life was took away,
An accident as he drove home, from work that awful day.
And despite the life that Andrew lived, so honourable and true,
I find it so regrettable that Christ he never knew.......Amen.

CHOICE

Do you think this world will miss you, when
your days on Earth are through?
Will they build some lasting monument, so they remember you?
Have you really made an impact, that everyone can see,
Will your name live on, when you are gone, will that be your legacy?

Although we'd like to think so, that won't be the case,
For life has taught there's someone else out there to take our place.
Although your friends and family, may
break their hearts to see you go,
How about the others that you've never come to know?

To them you were a stranger, and just another face,
Another headstone resting in a dark and lonely place.
But there's one I know will miss you, it will cut Him like a knife,
The one who took it on Himself, and granted you a life.

He sees how you have used it, and everything you've done,
He knows if you've accepted Christ, the Father and the Son.
He gives us all the gift of choice, to accept Him or decline,
And I pray the choice that you have made,
will be the same as mine....Amen.

PAID IN FULL

He's beside me as I walk in death's dark vale,
He's the strength I need when I am old and frail,
He is the wind that fills my sails, He's always there and never fails,
And I know it was for me, He took those nails.

Notwithstanding all the pain of Calvary,
He opened up His arms and welcomed me,
Were I to catalogue my sin, I do not know where I'd begin
He removed my scales so I was made to see.

Though He implored His Father at Gethsemane,
To ask please Father take this cup from me.
With such obedience from a Son, to ensure His Fathers will be done,
But He already knew the answer to His plea.

And even in the pain that He went through,
He said forgive them for they know not what they do.
And all of Heaven must have cried, when
they heard how He had died.
To pay for both the sins of me and you.....Amen.

REWARD

I draw my greatest pleasure. from a love beyond all measure,
Worth much more to me than jewels or gold.
It holds all that I believe, it's the very air I breath,
It's the greatest possession I will ever hold.

It's what keeps me going on, it's what my hopes are pinned upon,
It's what makes the blood keep flowing through my veins,
Father, Son and Holy Ghost, comprise the things I value most,
You can take away all else while this remains.

And when my days on Earth are through, I'll be granted life anew,
As I'm lifted to my mansion in the sky,
Where I will dwell for evermore, with all of those who went before,
And the Lord will wipe away the tears I cry.

I will bathe in golden light, as I don my robes of white,
And wear a crown of Glory on my head,
All because I was set free, when my Jesus died for me,
And I clung every word He ever said......Amen.

OUR GOD IS ETERNAL

While the high and mighty tumble, and Empires start to crumble,
And the balance of power keeps swinging to and fro,
Forever and a day, the grace of God is here to stay,
And the love of God will always be on show.

Don't you believe it very strange, the way
the seasons chop and change,
Yet the God we have is constant and the same.
How His throne remains on High, while all the others wilt and die,
How Eternal is the power of His name.

While withered trees produce no fruit, the word of God is resolute,
And the Bible has withstood the test of time.
Trends and Fashions fizzle out, firm beliefs give way to doubt,
Yet His word contains a message so sublime.

And while we journey far and near, to just retain some souvenir,
Nothing gives the confidence He can.
But depending on our state, our hopes and dreams evaporate,
Still I know some day, He'll help me understand....Amen.

JESUS IS THE WAY

It's not so much religion, that makes a sinner new,
It's not attending church each week, although that's nice to do,
It's not by all the deeds we do, or how we refrain from sin.
It's simply opening up your heart, and letting Jesus in.

The only route to Heaven, is though the Saviour Christ,
And only when you've gave your heart, will you have paid the price,
Impressing some by telling them, just what they want to hear,
Those empty words mean nothing, unless they are sincere.

Some may try to tell you, there's conditions to be met,
Some debt to pay, some words to say, but all of these forget,
The blood of Jesus paid the bill, at Calvary that day,
And through the sacrifice He made, He swept our sins away.

The road to Heaven's open, and the wind is set to fair,
You only need to follow Him and He will lead you there.
Forget about the trappings, that man has put in place,
Jesus Christ is all we need, through His Amazing Grace...Amen

HE'S THERE

When your world's collapsing round you and everything you touch,
When the pressure's really mounting, or
the strain becomes too much.
When you're fighting back the current, but the water's on the rise,
When it was you who made the effort, but
some other claims the prize.

When the friends you had desert you, or
break the promises they made,
When you need a little sunshine, but it rains on your parade.
When the problems start to multiply, more than you could realise,
And the help so badly needed, never seems to materialise.

That's the time we need someone, to lead us through the pain,
To lift us up from where we lie, unto our feet again.
When the hole is getting deeper, and we're sinking further down,
There's just the one sure method, of turning things around.

Look towards the Saviour, call to Him today,
Search and you will find Him, He's never far away.
Cast your eyes to Jesus, His is the hand to which I clutched,
You will feel His love surround you, and you'll
know that you've been touched...Amen.

MY TESTIMONY

Every nerve was tingling, from my head down to my feet,
As the Pastor read my name aloud and I arose from off my seat.
I was somehow carried forward, made my way up to the stage,
With my Testimony ready, neatly typed on every page.

I'm sure my lip was trembling, and everybody knew,
But I also felt my love of God, would somehow see me through.
The first words were the hardest, and I struggled at the start,
But I had to tell the story, that lay hidden in my heart.

It felt like there were thousands, all there and watching me,
But in truth just maybe thirty, was the true reality.
So I told how Jesus changed me, when He came into my life,
As the eyes of those who listened, almost pierced me like a knife.

But the Holy Ghost was there with me, when I needed Him so much,
His presence right in front of me, that I could almost touch.
He took away my nervousness, made my anxiety to flee
As I got to tell the story, of how Lord Jesus rescued me....Amen

THE WELL

When God above looks down on us, I wonder what He sees,
There's an awful lot to anger Him and not a lot to please,
I'm pretty sure He's sorrowful, when He sees how we behave,
In spite of what He did for us, when His only Son He gave.

It's not like we don't even know, the hurt we're causing Him,
For the one who sent his Son to die, with nails in every limb.
So I ask myself the question, how selfish can one get?
That the Cross, the blood, the sacrifice, we're happy to forget,

And then we call upon His name, whenever things go wrong,
And by His mercy He steps in, as He's done all along.
And do we take the time to thank, for the help that He sends down?
No, not a word until the next dilemma comes around,

We draw upon His mercy, like taking water from a well,
It may well be we're grateful, but do we take the time to tell?
The thought we have no gratitude, must make Him want to cry,
But we just keep drawing from His well,
until the well runs dry?....Amen.

THE WORD

The word of God's for sharing, as is the book from which it stemmed,
But if we keep it hidden, by our silence we're condemned.
It's the only weapon that we have, to counter Satan's claims.
And proclaim the name of Jesus, as the name above all names.

So many souls in peril, through unforgiven sins,
The World's forgot where lies all end, and where the truth begins.
Honesty's abandoned, with deception running rife,
As the lack of Faith we see these days, corrupts our way of life.

And we see the consequences, detrimental to our cost,
We must start to spread the word again, or we risk the message lost.
For that's the least that we can do, to keep God's word alive,
It's the reason I have come so far, and helped me to survive.

In every town and City, let us spread the message round,
That only through the word of God, is true salvation found,
We need to shout it constantly, we need to shout it clear,
That the Lord is coming back again, and the
moments drawing near....Amen.

FREED

I sampled Earthly pleasures, when my life was unfulfilled,
They promised me such happiness, but nothing ever did.
They were not as they were advertised, and brought me only grief.
For in the end, they offered, only temporary relief.

The drugs induced a feeling, I was floating in the air,
But when I awoke next morning, all the problems were still there,
The alcohol brought numbness, and helped to ease the pain,
But when I set the bottle down, they all returned again.

I was searching for an answer, and trying to find a cure,
As to what could fill this hole in me, and I really wasn't sure.
But I'd never even thought of God, why would He want me?
Until I'd exhausted every other possibility.

So I opened up a Bible, and I began to read,
And in it's pages, there I found, the solution that I need.
I read of Jesus sacrifice, when I thought my battle lost,
And the hole in me was filled again, because
of Calvary's cross....Amen.

CONTROL

Evil is advancing, with goodness in retreat,
Selfishness takes over, when we're staring at defeat.
It seems these days, that man's prepared to sell his very soul,
Yet I take my consolation, Knowing God is in control.

Deception's now the normal and honesty is dead,
At every opportunity, evil lifts it's head.
We've somehow missed the target, of having Heaven as our goal,
Yet I take my consolation, knowing God's still in control.

War keeps raging round us, there never seems to be a lull,
Churches now are empty, that not long ago were full.
Faith has been abandoned, but God's not lost His hold,
So I take my consolation, knowing He's still in control.

The darkest hour will always be, the one before the dawn,
It's in the light of Jesus Christ, my hopes are resting on.
This fractured World will be repaired, the Lord will make it whole,
And all will see, eventually, that God was in control...Amen.

GOING HOME

There'll be transparent rivers flowing, And a Rainbow in the sky,
There'll be a million voices singing, sending praise to God on high.
There'll be cries of celebration, as the bells begin to ring,
As we kneel in adoration, in the presence of our King.

We will meet with friends and family, by a crystal clear lagoon,
The ones, that once we all believed, were took away too soon.
There'll be no more pain and sorrow, we will leave them all behind,
There'll be family for the orphan, there'll be eyesight for the blind.

There'll be no more war or hunger, when
we reach that Promised Land,
There'll be no divided Nations, just one brotherhood of man.
There will be no need for passports with no borders or frontiers,
There'll be no more cause for worry, there'll
be no more cause for tears.

And all of this will come to pass, yes, all of this and more,
My descriptions can't do justice, to the things that lie in store.
My Saviour gave His life for me, to show how much He cared,
And soon He'll come to lead us home, to the
place that He's prepared...Amen.

AMBASSADORS

For all professing Christians, wherever we may be,
We carry on our shoulders, great responsibility,
For others look upon us, and everything we do,
Then make their final judgement, in what they see in me and you.

So do they look with envy, or regard us all as fools,
Do they respect the faith we have, or hold to ridicule.
There's an onus placed upon us, and all we do and say,
To represent the God we love, in every single way.

We must display our honesty, to those we want to reach,
We must have firm commitment, in all we try to preach.
Remember we're ambassadors, for all that we believe,
So always be prepared to wear your heart upon your sleeve.

We must go forth as fishermen, casting out our net,
We must remember Calvary, and never let the World forget.
And if we practise what we preach, our nets will start to swell,
Then every soul we capture, will be one less bound for Hell.....Amen.

FAMILY

She was just a single Mother, but she did the best she could,
In trying to raise her son with pride, as every parent should.
The Father was a memory, from a long, long time ago,
For he heard that she was pregnant, and he didn't want to know.

But still she tried to fill his shoes, in every way she could,
And in a way enjoyed the stress and strains of parenthood.
Yet she knew her son was missing out, because he had no Dad,
And although she tried her very best, the thought still made her sad.

Then the conversation came around, between her and her son,
When she apologised most kids had two, when he had only one,
But her son then raised a finger, and stopped her in her tracks,
As he put his arms around her waist, as
they both fought their tears back.

I have a Father, mother, it just he dwells above,
I speak with Him quite often and He showers us with love,
I tell Him how we love Him, on behalf of you and me,
And as long as He abides with us, we've a perfect family....Amen.

RELATIONSHIP

It's a lonely road we travel, until we come to grips,
For we just get out what we put in. like all relationships.
But we need to keep on building, having Jesus as our friend,
For when you give your life to Him, it's worth it in the end.

In the early days we struggle, and the going can be tough,
But He sends the willpower that we need,
when we don't have enough.
Perhaps it's easier quitting, and avoiding all the fuss,
'Til we recall the sacrifice, that He once made for us.

Just keep walking forward, the Lord will show the way,
And you'll find the road you've chosen, just gets easier day by day.
Keep your eyes on Jesus, and hold your head up high,
There's Angels watching over us, to help us all get by.

Your relationship will blossom, just as easy as you please.
The more you come to know Him, the more you'll feel at ease,
As long as we have Jesus, who could ask for more,
And you'll wonder why you didn't give
your life to Him before...Amen.

AWAKEN

It's no time to be complacent, there's a battle to be won,
But it rages not on battlefield, but deep in everyone.
It requires a lot of bravery, if we're truly to succeed,
But with Jesus as our Master, He'll attend to every need.

So do not let us slumber, we need warriors fast and strong,
Prepared to march to battle, to face the enemy head-on.
To wield a sword for Jesus, that will neither blunt nor rust,
And illuminate the darkness, with the truth He's given us.

Let us conquer all before us, in every place we go,
Let us win those hearts for Jesus, and watch His Kingdom grow.
There will be no time for resting, there is much to be endured,
But we'll find it so rewarding, when the victory is secured.

We will see our foes all scatter, as evil takes to flight,
And our hearts will be uplifted, when our Lord has won the fight.
And we'll all be clothed in splendour, all adorned in our white gowns,
As we kneel before our Master, to be
presented with our crowns....Amen.

STORMS

There may be storms to conquer, but this I've come to know,
It takes a little rain sometimes to make the Harvest grow.
And the darkest hour they tell us, is just before the dawn,
So no matter how it seems just now, we must keep pressing on.

You can overcome the obstacles that life puts in your way,
You can put your past behind you, start to live for each new day.
There's a way to ease your burdens, no matter how it seems,
There's a way to end your nightmares, and realise your dreams.

When the odds are stacked against you,
there's only one way you can win,
That's to open up your heart to Him, and let the Saviour in.
He can turn the rain to sunshine, and brighten up your days,
He can help to ease your burdens, in so many different ways.

But best of all He'll bring you hope, a rock to lean upon,
He'll bring a purpose to your life, a reason to go on.
He'll lift you from the doldrums, make the Sun to shine again,
Have you soaring like an eagle, and put
an end to all your pain...Amen.

RENEWED

There was a life renewed, to the way it
should, that hour I first believed,
Enriched and given purpose, more than even I conceived.
How His light illuminated the darkest corner of my soul,
How He took the pieces of my life and somehow made me whole.

Despite all my transgressions, There you stood with open arms,
You welcomed me, you set me free, you've sheltered me from harm.
You've given me, new dignity, I've felt your loving Grace,
You bore the scars at Calvary, 'twas there you took my place.

When I raised my hand in acknowledgement,
and took you for my King,
I never really understood, the Blessings you would bring.
For I was so unworthy, just a sinner so unclean,
But still you showed acceptance, led me to pastures green.

And all I am I owe to you, and I give my adoration,
For you placed a flame within my heart, made me a new creation.
I asked and you accepted me, now my life is not the same,
So for all the time you grant to me, I'll praise your Holy name…Amen.

UNASHAMED

I will glorify the Lord I love wherever I may be,
And sing my praises to His name, so unashamedly.
I will testify to all I meet, the things He's done for me,
I'll urge them to accept him too, without apology.

And after all I tell them, if their views remain the same.
Then when they stand before His throne,
there'll be no-one else to blame.
When the Book of Life is opened, and their name's not on the list,
Maybe then they'll understand, the opportunity they missed.

For we only get one chance at life, you must make up your mind,
There isn't any button, to let us cancel or rewind.
Lives are being measured, from Sunrise until Sunset,
Make sure you use it wisely, it's the only one you'll get.

So listen for Him calling, then accept His wondrous news,
Or you'll wake up someday to find, your chances have been used.
There's just one path to Heaven, and that Eternal life it brings,
That's acceptance of our Saviour. The Almighty King of Kings…Amen.

IT'S YOU

It's you that I find comfort in, when things go badly wrong,
From you I draw my confidence, when it feels I don't belong.
It's you who always listens, without casting any blame,
And you provide the answer, when I call upon your name.

It's you who guides this life of mine, by giving me directions,
And only you can understand, my thoughts and words and actions.
In you I find forgiveness, irrespective of the crime,
You welcome me with open arms, you forgive me every time.

It's you who went to Calvary, and there you took my place,
It's you who died and rose again, through God's amazing Grace.
It was you who took the punishment, before they watched you die,
And all of this you done my Lord, for as sinner such as I.

If they asked me what you mean to me, where would I begin?
You were the Lamb without a blemish, and completely free from sin.
If they asked me how I'm come this far, my answer would be true,
If I had to give a reason Lord, that answer would be you....Amen.

HE IS RISEN

He is risen, I'm forgiven, He broke the chains to set the prisoner free,
He bore the pain, but rose again, and
conquered death to claim the victory.
He'll come below, He told us so, to claim
His rightful place upon the throne,
And all will see, His majesty, the time approaches
when the trumpet has been blown.

And how I pray, I'll see that day, as every
nation comes to bow the knee,
Please let it be, my Lord I'll see, to thank
Him for how much he did for me.
For all His care, for being there, for His love of just a sinner such as I,
For Calvary, for loving me, For the strength
He sends in helping me get by.

We'll see His face, we'll feel His Grace, as He
leads His children to that promised Land,
Oh what a story, we're bound for Glory, to a
place the human mind can't understand.
And before our eyes, the dead will rise, and we'll
see again the ones we miss so much,
His promise kept, for those who slept, reborn
again because of Jesus touch.

For nothings unbelievable, and nothings unachievable,
as long as we have Jesus by our side,
So please be strong, it won't be long, He's
coming as the groom and we His bride.
Because of all He thought of us, because He cared so much
for us, He gave His life to show how much He cared,
And I know that He's aware, I sent my message in a prayer,
to let Him know His children are prepared....Amen.

HE'S COMING

I see a World in poverty, and ask the question why?
So many sit in silence, as this world begins to die.
I see suffering beyond belief, and my heart could almost burst,
And I ask myself what happened to the world that God gave us?

When I think of how things used to be, I find it really hard,
That a thing of so much beauty, could be so brutalised and scarred.
Instead of making progress, that I believe we should,
We seem to make a better job of wrecking all that's good.

I can't say it surprises me, for this was all foretold,
That men would turn their backs on God, and worship only gold.
And now I see this taking place, just like the Bible said,
Where once we witnessed beauty, there is war and death instead.

I only pray we realise, the end is drawing near,
Jesus Christ is coming soon, the time is almost here.
My hopes and dreams are resting, in the Saviour I have found,
I only pray you find him too, before the trumpet sounds....Amen

KING OF KINGS

King of Kings and Lord of Lords, the Master of my soul,
You took the pieces of my life, and somehow made me whole.
You took a worthless sinner, undeserving and unclean,
And taught me I had value, that up to then remained unseen,

You taught me how to stand again, when I was on my knees,
Purified this sinners heart, that was riddled by disease.
You broke the chains that had me bound, as if they were not there,
Opened up my prison cell and led me from despair,

I thought I never needed you, but how wrong could I be,
My life a mere existence, but you gave New Life to me.
I was living in oblivion, I dwelt among the blind,
I was hiding in the shadows, but you took the time to find.

And what a wondrous difference, that day you set me free,
What a transformation Lord, when you accepted me.
King of Kings and Lord of Lords, the Master of my soul,
My world revolves around you now, and Heaven is my goal....Amen.

UNSEEING

There are limits to Mans knowledge, that's the way it's always been,
Mysteries still outstanding, and answers yet unseen.
But as long as we have God above, this world will still revolve,
He already holds the answers, that science cannot solve.

Sometimes it's much better, just to have a little trust,
It's difficult not knowing, but I feel sometimes we must.
The curtain will be lifted, and all knowledge put on show,
But only in the Lords good time, when He
thinks that we should know,

So until then, just keep trusting, and never let Him go,
Be thankful that the God we serve, is forever in control.
There is wisdom in the saying, that ignorance is bliss,
His grace is all sufficient, so just remember this.

I know someday He'll furnish us, with all we need to know,
And if we place our trust in Him, the truth will always show.
Yes, there's limits to Mans knowledge, and there will always be,
Until God removes what's blinding us, Then
every eye shall see....Amen.

JUST ASK

I may not know the details of the workings of your mind,
But I see the tracks on both your cheeks, your tears have left behind.
I can see the pain reflected, when I look into your eyes.
Even though you try to mask the grief, it's impossible to disguise.

The pillow that you slept upon, could tell me even more,
Still moist from the tears you left there, as you slept the night before,
I see right through that pain you feel, that you cover with a mask,
I can tell that your in need of help, but your just too proud to ask.

You bear such heavy burdens, that you carry on your own,
You wear a smile in company, that's not there when your alone.
You regret the independence, that's become a part of you,
But you'll never kid a kidder, for I have been there too.

If I could strip away the varnish, I could see what's really you,
And expose these instincts that I feel, and confirm that they are true,
I could point you to the one I found, when I lived my life the same,
The one who turned my life around, when
I called upon His name....Amen.

COMPASSION

If you've ever watched a Mother, caress her new born child,
That's the love that we experience, with Jesus by our side.
The love of God is special, it's the thing I value most,
The greatest gift that I possess, and nothing else comes close.

Hills we thought unclimbable, we take them in our stride,
Yes, nothing is impossible with Jesus by our side.
To those who've yet to find Him, with hearts so badly stained,
Just reach out and touch Him, for there's so much to be gained,

His arms are always open, if you'll come to Him today,
The Earthly things that keep us bound, Can all be swept away.
Dependencies can vanish, He can set the hostage free,
He'll re-ignite a spark in you, the way He did for me.

He can elevate and lift us, so we stand out from the crowds
If we're lying in the gutter, He can raise us to the clouds.
The God I serve's compassionate, so caring, warm and mild,
Just the way that Mother shows compassion for her child...Amen.

WITHOUT WALLS

The preacher did his very best, with the sermon that he preached,
But the church was filled with only those,
who already had been reached.
And those who needed God the most, were sitting nowhere near,
They did not visit church that day, so never got to hear.

He brought the service to an end, with another altar call,
And not a single hand was raised, throughout that Mission hall.
And when the final Hymn was sang, and the final prayer was prayed,
The congregation left for home, not remembering what was said.

I only tell this story, in the hope you'll understand,
There are countless souls in need of God, all throughout this Land,
Because they've yet to find the Lord, we never should condemn,
But if they refuse to come to church, then we must go to them.

We'll find them in the betting shops, the prisons or the Bar,
It's up to us to search them out no matter where they are.
We need to follow Jesus, and answer when he calls,
And this is just achievable, if we're Churches without walls....Amen.

ATTACKED

Thank God for our ability, to read between the lines,
For Jesus tries to capture hearts, while Satan targets minds,
But the devil offers promises of things that cannot be,
The Bible is the word of truth, and the truth will set us free.

Be thankful then we've Jesus, the name above all names,
The only one who's capable, of ending Satan's games.
There's nothing Satan throws at me, that I can't overcome.
My protection rests with God above, both Father and the Son,

But still he keeps on trying, to get inside my head,
Confusing me, and tempting me, with promises he's made.
He considers me a target, so my soul must be His aim,
But I counter every move he makes, when I mention Jesus name.

Because I am a child of God, he sees me as a threat,
But he was defeated once before and I won't let him forget.
I'll meet his challenge face to face, stand with him toe to toe,
The Lord's the owner of my heart, and will not let it go.....Amen.

IN THE BEGINNING

At the outset there was darkness, as black as any night,
Devoid of any shape or form, So God created light.
And out of total darkness, Man was made to see,
The splendour of the God we serve, in all His majesty.

So, if each life is a candle, that's ignited at our birth,
But constantly it burns away, just like our time on Earth.
I wonder would there come a point, when
our flame becomes so dim,
That we'd realise we only shine, as long as we have Him.

For a gentle breeze is all we need, to make the flame go out,
But the love of God will shelter us, of that I have no doubt.
We must shine a light for Jesus, the Life, the Truth, the Way,
Illuminate the darkness, until we turn night into day.

Lets all stand together, so the very Heavens glow,
Burn so bright that all the Earth, will see our light and know,
That darkness has be banished, so that every eye can see,
Then every candle on the Earth, can burn eternally....Amen.

FAILURE

We fall short of your Glory Lord, seven days each week,
We're a million miles and growing, from the target that you seek,
We sin through our own volition, not as victims of duress,
Yet in spite of this, our Father, you don't love us any less.

So I ask myself one question, with my hand held to my heart,
Is it purely down to selfishness, or weakness on our part,
Are we really so incapable, of doing as you ask,
Do we surrender far to easily, at the prospect of the task.

For after all, we have a choice, in most things that we do,
But because of how we fail each day, we stray away from you.
Our sin must feel like arrows, that can pierce your very heart,
Yet still you shower us with your love, no anger on your part.

Your prepared to keep on giving, while we're content to take,
And you tell us you'll forgive us, after each mistake we make,
You offer us your guidance, yet we fail in every task,
But still you'll grant Eternity, if we're prepared to ask....Amen

EVERYWHERE

You may have many siblings, or been born an only child,
You may live in a City, or in the countryside,
But you won't have far to travel, to hear the word of God,
His presence is attainable, wherever we may we trod.

You may not have a local church, and do not drive a car,
But Our Lord is ever present, no matter where you are.
Forget about surroundings, He'll hear each word you said,
You don't need a Cathedral, simply kneel beside your bed.

For where one or two are gathered, He is in their midst,
And no praise that we send to Him, will ever be dismissed.
If you really want to Honour God, you won't have far to roam,
If you should ask, He'll come to you, in the comfort of your home.

And before the hands can indicate, a second on the clock,
He'll be right there in front of you, just listen for His knock.
Open up your heart to Him, and He will enter in,
If you call His name then He'll appear, the forgiver of our sin....Amen.

LEAN ON ME

Lean on me when storms appear and I'll be waiting there,
Call to me in times of need and I will hear your prayer.
Follow me when you are lost, in mountain, valley, field.
Trust in me when danger comes, and I will be your shield.

Look to me for guidance, whenever your in doubt,
If Satan ever threatens you, let me cast him out.
Ask and you'll be given, I'll meet your every need.
Depend on me, when others fail, I'll help you to succeed.

If rain clouds gather overhead, It's I who'll clear the skies,
When life becomes to much for you. I'm there to dry your eyes,
I'm there to bring you comfort, if your temper should erupt,
If you should ever trip and fall, I'm there to lift you up.

In me you'll find forgiveness, always have and always will,
I sent my Son to Calvary, and there He paid the bill.
You only have to trust in me, and you'll be truly Blessed,
Only deal with what you can, and I will do the rest....Amen.

THE WORD IS TRUTH

When we sugar-coat the gospel, we do more harm than good,
We need to share it word for word, and tell it as we should.
Some may well be frightened by the story that we tell,
But I would scare them into Heaven, before
I'd watch them march to Hell.

I refuse to make apologies for speaking what is true,
For I only follow Jesus, and the things He asks me to.
I believe it's just dishonest, and we don't give our best,
If we just share the pretty bits, and disregard the rest.

I'll refer to what is written, for that's where truth is found,
And no matter how untenable, I will not water down.
For if I add or take away then others might refute,
But when I use the word of God, then there is no dispute.

So don't let others tell you, and never be deceived,
There are stories out there going round, that should not be believed.
I only use the word of God, all else would be perverse,
And The Bible is the word of God, every
chapter, word and verse...Amen.

YOU MATTER

You may feel insignificant, your life a throwaway.
That none would ever miss you if you left this world today.
Invisible and worthless, unworthy in extreme,
The one who's always still asleep, while others live their dream.

But God sees something different, for He created you,
And He'll ensure your light will shine, whenever time is due,
He made you for a purpose, your included in His plan,
For He made us in His image, every woman, child and man.

As part of God's creation, we can shape each passing day,
Each and everyone of us, have all a role to play.
From the most mature to the youngest child, everyone will fit,
But it won't happen overnight, and we have to work at it.

You may not share the spotlight, but you're waiting in the wings,
To share the love of God around, and everything that brings.
So maybe when you reach that stage, you'll take a different view,
When you understand, Almighty's plan,
and how it needed you....Amen.

I BELIEVE

You tell me you have faith in God, if so, then answer this,
If there is a God, then why allow, such evil to exist?
If God is so forgiving, filled with passion, full of Grace,
Why does He sit idly by, and watch it all take place?

A fair and honest question, that deserves a fair reply,
I really can't explain it but I'll do my best to try.
God keeps holding out His hand, but we just walk away,
We've turned our backs towards Him and we've lost the will to pray.

We hide Him from our children, we can't mention Him in schools
We used to live by his commands, but then we changed the rules.
The evil that we see today, does not stem from above,
But because we turn our backs on God, and pushed away His love.

I know God's heart is breaking, by the tears that fill His eyes,
But it was us who made the vacuum, that Satan occupies
We've gave this world to evil, without the need for theft.
And that's why I believe in God, He's the
only hope that's left.....Amen.

UNBURDENED

When the game is all but finished, and there's no more cards to play,
And you feel it's time to lock the door, and throw the key away.
When the World's collapsing round you, and the well is almost dry,
When your burdens are so troublesome, all you can do is cry.

Then who can offer succour, I believe there's only one,
Cast you eyes, towards the skies, from whence your help will come.
Hope is found in Jesus, it was for you He paid the cost.
The outcast and the lonely, the suffering and lost,

He can introduce you to a life, that you have never known,
He'll give you back your dignity, through the seeds that He has sown.
He'll touch that aching heart of yours, and nullify the pain,
Re-construct the life you had, so you are born again.

There's joy in living life again, with Jesus by your side,
How you ever lived without Him, will leave you mystified.
And once you've come to know Him, you'll never let Him go,
He'll be there to lift and carry you, like no-one else I know...Amen.

THE RETURN

What if Jesus Christ came back tomorrow, would
you see it as an answer to your prayer?
Would you raise your arms to welcome His returning,
or need some extra time to be prepared?
When the trumpet sounds and clouds begin to
open, will joyous celebration fill your heart?
For you must have known this day was going to happen,
for He promised us away back at the start.

He told us in His promise He's returning, and
now I feel that time is drawing near,
The question is were we prepared to listen, for if
we did there's nothing we should fear.
The day of our salvation is approaching, and
what a wondrous sight we'll get to see,
As every Nation gathers in His presence, and
without exception, all will bow the knee.

The King of Kings and Lord of Lords is coming, to
take His rightful place upon the throne,
And all will see His Majesty and Glory,
whenever He returns to lead us home.
Heaven's bells will ring as loud as thunder,
Angel choirs will offer up their praise.
And nothing that has happened up to present,
could equal that the most glorious of days.

I realise the time is of His choosing, but all
the signs I see would indicate,
That some day soon we're going to see our Master,
the only thing that's missing is the date.
But I know beyond a doubt that I am ready,
whenever He decides the time is right,
I'll be waiting with my brothers and my sisters, when the
clouds disperse and He comes into sight...Amen.

PRAYER

The power of Prayer is wonderful, but experience will show,
That when we send our prayer to God, the answer's sometimes No.
I'm sure He has His reasons, and I truly understand,
That He always knows what's best for us, much more than any man.

Our Father always listens and every prayer is heard,
And even when He answers no, He's showing us He cared.
In every way I realise, how richly I've been blessed,
And I put my Faith in God above, and trust that He knows best.

How could I be angry, with the one who gave His Son?
Who knew me in my Mothers womb before my life begun.
So if He turns down my request, I won't hold Him to blame,
I'll carry on regardless, with my love for Him the same,

I may look back in times to come, and see that He was right,
For refusing what I prayed for, for He knew what lay in sight.
It's then I'll send my thanks in prayer, to the God who set me free,
For deciding what was right and wrong, in
the plans He held for me....Amen.

ASK

Another day, another struggle, yet another war to fight,
If this is how you live your life, then something isn't right.
Has your home became your prison, perhaps
your world has lost it's shape,
And it's only in your sleeping hours, your finding your escape.

Do you live in isolation, as you face each new affray?
Do you dread the thought of company, is it easier that way?
Do you long to see the Sun again, if only for a while,
Are you comfortable when crying, but can't remember how to smile,

Life can be a struggle, we all have our ups and downs,
Every day is not a circus, with the candy-floss and clowns.
But the Lord provides the answer, when the skies above are grey,
For He knows, we need a little help as we move from day to day.

Put your faith in Jesus Christ, if your living life like this,
He can bring you back to life again and restore the things you miss,
Why prolong the misery, when you know there's help at hand,
Put your trust in Jesus, only He can understand...Amen.

DRAWING CLOSER

No more books to balance, no more bill to pay,
When Jesus went to Calvary, He swept my sins away,
All my living nightmares, now replaced by pleasant dreams,
Joy and laughter's took the place, of the heartaches and the screams.

No more cause to worry, and no more fear of death,
Just knowing I will be with Him when I take my final breath.
He'll be waiting there to meet me, and place His hand in mine,
As a feeling washes over me, that words can not define,

There'll be throngs of Angels singing, in robes of brilliant white,
As I behold, those streets of gold, Oh what a wondrous sight.
And all because I listened, when He called out my name,
My Sin has been forgiven, and I'm free of guilt and shame.

The doubts that once kept me awake, by now have disappeared,
Now I know the road that lies ahead is much better that I feared,
The years may try to take their toll, but death has lost it's sting,
For every one that passes, brings me closer to my King......Amen.

CLEANSED

Look into that heart of yours, that pumps blood through your veins,
Can you see the damage sin has done, do you recognise the stains?
Each evil thought we sanction, and poor decision we have made,
Contributes to the problem and turns our heart a darker shade.

Sin is like a cancer, and we need to be aware,
Just because we cannot see it, doesn't mean it isn't there.
It multiplies so quickly as it spreads like forest fire.
It drags us down, confuses us, and drags us through the mire,

But there's good news in the offing, where sin can taste defeat,
That hope is found in Jesus Christ, whenever our paths meet.
He's the only one that's capable of turning lives around,
For only in the arms of Christ is true forgiveness found,

He'll cleanse the very darkest heart, remove each blackened cell,
Renew, forgive, invigorate, and save us all from Hell.
He'll take away the sin we bore and lead to pastures green,
But only when He's touched us, is our
heart completely clean…Amen.

PRAISE HIM

If a ship's to leave the harbour, it's anchor must be raised,
And if we're to earn the love of God, I believe He must be praised,
Respectfully and with honour, each and every day,
For all that He has done for us, and a debt we can't repay.

To think He sent His Son to die, that sinners might be free,
To understand the suffering and the blood He shed for me,
The depth of love He held for us, His passion and desire,
Then to watch His life just ebb away, like the embers of a fire.

But then there came the morning, at the dawn of that third day,
Our Saviour brought to life again, when the stone was rolled away.
His Resurrection, made the pain, much easier to bear,
But Calvary must have left it's mark, on all who witnessed there.

The empty tomb bears evidence, He was the Son of Man,
And I try to show my gratitude in every way I can,
I'm grateful for forgiveness and all salvation gives,
But most all I'm grateful in the knowledge He still lives...Amen

WHICH?

A captive or a captor, which do you prefer?
The one behind the prison bars or the one who placed him there.
And which one is the prisoner, by looking we can't tell,
Who is on the outside or the inside of the cell?

It may well be, the two we see, adhere to different views,
The one in chains accepted Christ, while his guard has yet to choose.
In that case who has freedom, it's the prisoner for me,
He may have lost his liberty, but gained eternity.

The convicts been forgiven, though he's guilty of the crime,
While one day soon, the guard may find, that he's run out of time.
When Jesus Christ accepts us, we have everything we need,
And if we're forgiven by the Son, we're truly free indeed.....Amen.

IGNORED

You may have heard the word of God, but foolishly ignored,
You may have even sat in church, uncomfortable and bored.
You may have owned a Bible, but never found the time to read,
You may have heard as Jesus called, but never felt the need.

You may have even known the Lord, but regrettably backslid,
You may have knew you needed Him, but kept your feelings hid.
But when I look into your eyes, it makes it very plain,
You wish that you could turn back time, and live your life again.

For here you stand at Heavens gate, dejected and forlorn,
Regretting how you lived your life, with a heart so badly torn.
If only you had listened, if you'd answered Jesus call,
It could have been so different, you could have had it all.

But time has now caught up with you, and judgement lies ahead,
It's too late now, you can't retract, the things you did and said.
We only get one shot at life, and this you always knew.
Now I must leave you with a prayer, that's all that I can do....Amen

LABELS

Religion's just a label, that tears us all apart,
But the love of God, a relationship, that forms within a heart.
We may mock the other churches, that bear a different name,
But then again they look at ours, and do the very same.

Division stems from Satan, and Unity from Christ,
If I could only mend the wounds, I'd happily pay the price.
And then all man-made differences, we could put aside,
One church, one congregation, one people unified.

We could all exalt the God we love, as we sit with one another,
And treat the person next to us, like a Sister or a Brother.
The blood of Christ would bind us, there'd be no more disarray,
One bride of Christ awaiting Him, to carry us away.

If only we possessed the will, to make this dream come true,
Then you could sit in church with me, and I could sit with you,
How glorious a day we'd see, as the bells would ring out loud,
And Heaven could then celebrate, that
we've made Jesus proud....Amen

RELEASE

Disputes can leave us angry, and battles leave us scarred,
Sometimes life can smother us and we find the going hard.
When we feel it would be easier just giving up the ghost,
That's when knowing Jesus Christ can benefit us most.

I used to live the same as you, each day was filled with dread.
But life is just a stepping-stone, to the one that lies ahead.
And like a river we set forth, to face our destiny,
As we meander back and forth until we reach the sea.

But the wind affects our current, and may try to stem our flow,
And that's when we need Jesus Christ, Like no-one else I know.
At every point along our path, He'll ensure that we flow free.
He'll calm the winds ahead of us, 'til we reach the estuary.

And when we reach that Sea of Life, He's waiting by the shore,
To receive us at that golden beach, where pain will be no more.
Yet another river's found it's course, as a sinner's plucked from Hell,
May many rivers congregate until the ocean's swell...Amen.

MY PRAYER

Thank you Lord for loving me when I thought that no-one could,
Thank you for your sacrifice upon that Cross of Wood,
Thank you my Redeemer, that you died to set me free,
Thank you Holy Spirit, that you still abide in me,

If you will guide my footsteps, I will follow where I'm led,
Let me keep my eyes upon you Lord, and focus straight ahead.
Lead me unto Glory, cover me with Grace,
For you promised I could be with you, that you've prepared a place.

Always be beside me Lord, through the sunshine and the rain,
Be my staff in times of need, and safeguard me from pain,
In a world of such division, that's consumed by greed and pride,
Bring me through the storms of life, and out the other side.

And in return I'll give my heart, please take it Lord, it's yours,
So I may come and worship you, for as long as time endures.
And when I stand at Heaven's gates, I pray that it can be,
That the heart I gave, and the Faith I hold,
provide me with the key...Amen.

WHY

How trivial the reasons, why nations go to war,
How wasteful that we loose our young, and what their dying for.
How merciless we take a life, for an extra mile of land,
That we'd maim and kill for something, even we don't understand.

We were taught to love our enemies, and never harbour blame,
Yet still we seem to go to war, and fight in Jesus' name.
So did we really listen when He asked us to forgive?
Then why engage in conflict when there's a better way to live?

Will the arms we bear be silenced, will the fighting ever cease?
Will we recognise the Lord was right, for then we'll find true peace.
This mixed up generation, have lived in Satan's curse,
It's time to bring it to a halt, before it gets much worse.

It's time we turned to God again, and let our World be cured,
So our children don't inherit, all the things that we endured,
Then the bombs and bullets reigning down, can be replaced by love,
As peace descends on Earth again, our gift from up above...Amen

THE POWER AND THE GLORY

The God I serve works miracles, the only one who can.
Creator of the Universe, He breathed life into man.
He's above all understanding, with a love that's so divine,
And the thought He cares so much for me,
sends shivers down my spine.

Though all of us are sinners, He love's us all the same.
I bow my head in reverence, at the mention of His name.
Eternity looked dark for me, before the Lord I knew,
But now I know where I have been and where I'm going to.

Eternity became assured, when Jesus Christ was sent,
Forgiveness can be yours and mine, so long as we repent.
He doesn't ask a lot of us, there's no-one He'll rebuff,
Just that we place our trust in Him, and that alone's enough.

All our questions will be answered, our mysteries revealed,
The lost will be reclaimed by Him, the sick will all be healed,
We'll find rewards immeasurable, as His promises are kept,
And all of this within our reach, by taking that first step....Amen.

DOUBT

If ever you feel worthless or completely out of touch,
Remember Jesus died for you, He cared for you so much.
He took that cup of sorrow, and held it to His lip,
His arms are ever open, He'll never let you slip.

You are created in the image of the God of Abraham,
And both the world and Universe are resting in His palm.
So if you think your undeserving, that is far from true,
For He sent His Son to Calvary, to bleed and die for you.

Yes every soul is precious in the eyes of God above,
Beyond all comprehension is the measure of His love.
So, put away all thoughts you hold, that you're beyond His care,
You only have to call to Him and He is always there.

He's mended countless broken hearts, He gives the weary rest,
He knows the sin we're guilty of, but sees in us our best.
Take the time to talk with Him, He'll listen as you speak,
You'll find all that your searching for, He's
the answer that you seek.....Amen.

NEW LIFE

The moment that He touched me, I became a different man,
A desire was born within my heart to be part of Jesus' plan.
With the Holy Spirit guiding me, and showing me the way,
And the love I held for Jesus, getting stronger every day.

I was aware I was a sinner, and I knew I must repent,
But forgiveness can be found in me, was the message that He sent.
Were I to list the debt I owe, just where would I begin,
So, heavy was that price He paid, to wash away my sin.

There comes a moment in our lives, when He speaks to everyone,
And if you haven't heard Him yet, believe me it will come.
So make your preparations, for He's gave some thinking time,
But soon He'll ask the question and you must make up your mind.

Are you ready to receive Him, will you take His outstretched hand,
Will you give your heart to Jesus and become a different man.
You can put your past behind you, He'll forgive your every sin,
For it's only when you've found Him, that
your new life can begin....Amen

VICKY

If I were just a child again, less hardships would I face,
But I know my years have been betrayed by the wrinkles on my face.
Yet the lines you see, don't bother me,
they just mark the passing years,
The residue, that brought me through, both the laughter and the tears.

I reminisce about my life, the good times and the bad,
The friends I made, the things I said, and experiences I had.
I reflect on my decisions, where my mind was firmly set,
But then again the choices made, that I wish I could forget.

The Lord's been really kind to me, in every walk of life,
He's provided me, with stability, and the gift of a precious wife.
He listened to my every prayer, yet we'd sometimes disagree,
But overall He understood, just what was best for me.

And as I reach my golden years, These lines I will not hide,
For He's given me, the luxury, of someone by my side,
He took away the loneliness, as I wave goodbye to strife,
I thank you Lord for granting me, Victoria for my wife.....Amen.

FREE US

We are a privileged people, Lord let us not forget,
We can come into the House of God, free from fear or threat.
We can thank the only Son of God, that the love He gives is free,
While others risk their very lives, having no such Liberty.

Yes, we can raise our voices, in word and song and sound
While others have to cower away, for fear of being found,
And the faith we have can be displayed, anywhere we choose,
While others rot in prison cells, for holding different views.

If only we could share with them, the freedom we enjoy,
So they could worship as they please, without their lives destroyed.
But maybe through the love of God, by His power and His grace.
Someday soon we'll get to see, a miracle take place.

Our persecutors then will learn, how futile was their fight,
As we emerge from out the shadows, and stand proudly in the light.
This is what we pray for Lord, please set your people free,
But until that day, we'll stand with them, in solidarity....Amen.

GOD CALLING

If you listen very carefully, you may well hear a voice,
That's imploring you and telling you it's time to make a choice.
Everyone receives this call, and this is now your day,
So clear your mind and listen, put all other thoughts away.

Decisions tend to rule our lives, where there's many things at stake
But this is the most important one, that you will ever make.
Your past can be forgiven, your future be assured,
Temptation can be overcome and your weaknesses be cured.

You need to have a little faith in the one who died for you.
You only need to listen so His message can come through.
You'll recognise His gentle tone, that He's hoping you'll obey,
For when He's calling out to you, this is what He'll say.

For too long I've been looking on, while Satan's had you bound,
But I am here to let you know, there's new life to be found.
From there it's really up to you, what you do or say,
You can take the hand I offer you, or simply walk away....Amen.

RAIN

The days are getting colder now, and the evenings growing dark,
No longer do I waken up to the singing of the lark.
Summer has abandoned us, and the Winter's here again,
As the warmth that I enjoyed so much, is now replaced by rain,

But there's nothing like a Saviours love, to keep the spirit warm,
Since that first day of Creation, when He gave this Earth it's form.
Another year has come and gone, but a new one's just begun,
As the Earth completes it's yearly circuit all around the Sun.

This World will keep rotating, as the seasons come and go,
For we need the rain of Winter, just to make the harvest grow.
That's why I never get upset at the prospect of the rain,
I'll welcome every little drop, 'til the Lord comes back again...Amen.

REGRET

It could have been so different, if only then I'd knew,
That every word the Bible said was genuine and true,
If only I had listened to all the scriptures said,
I could have been in Heaven, but now I'm here instead.

I cannot say I wasn't told, I just refused to hear,
I chose the world, and not the Lord, and that's why I am here.
A Paradise was offered if I had followed Christ,
But foolishly I didn't and now I pay the price.

For all those reckless years I had, the women, wine and song,
I'm now condemned to darkness in the place that I belong.
My sin went unforgiven, How foolish could I be,
If only I had asked the Lord, He would have heard my plea.

But maybe now you've heard my tale, you'll choose a different way,
You'll maybe learn from my mistakes, and see the light of day.
This warning that I give to you, I trust you won't forget,
For those who die without the Lord, have Forever to regret...Amen.

HE'S COMING

At the end of days, when the trumpet sounds,
are you sure that you'll be spared?
Will Jesus come and carry you to the place that He's prepared?
Will you see the Nations gathered, what a sight that's going to be,
Will you stand before the Son of God, and humbly bend the knee?.

Do you believe the Lord's returning, have you given Him your heart?
Do you long to hear that trumpet blast, as the clouds begin to part?
Have you made your preparations, is your love for Jesus true?
For any day He's coming back, the time is overdue.

The puzzles near completion, all the pieces are in place,
Our Lord will walk on Earth again, through God's amazing Grace.
All His children will be gathered, from wherever they may roam,
As He leads us all to Glory to our new Eternal home.

Heavens Gates will open up as Jesus claims His bride,
There'll be cries of celebration, as He welcomes us inside.
The prophecy's unfolding, getting closer by the day,
Some are ready, some are not, but He's coming anyway....Amen.

FORGIVENESS MATTERS

I'm sorry for the things I said, for the cruelty that was me,
If only I could turn back time, I'd do things differently.
I'm sorry for my actions, when you treated me so well,
I'm sorry for upsetting you, and for every tear that fell.

But words are only sounds we make, and you and I both know,
That I used all my excuses, a long, long time ago,
But if there was any other way, to penetrate your heart,
Then I would surely find it, so we could make another start.

But I know I've caused you anguish, and some scars may never heal,
But I took this opportunity, to tell you how I feel.
I know the Lords forgiven me, that much I know is true,
And I pray you find it in your heart, so you'll forgive me too....Amen.

CAPTAIN AND MASTER

Our Faith becomes the anchor, that will not let us slip,
And Jesus is the captain, and the Master of the ship.
The storms we face may do their best to bring us to our knees,
But in His hands there rests the power, to calm the roughest seas.

Our journey may be perilous, but we are in safe hands,
For the captain we sail under, the very wind He does command.
The elements can pose no threat, to those who sail with him,
As thunder storms grow silent, and lightning just grows dim.

We will follow where He leads us, as our sails begin to sway,
But we won't need a compass, for I'm sure He knows the way.
We are headed to a harbour, where our friends have went before,
Where those we thought that we had lost, we'll get to see once more.

And when our vessel comes to rest, then we will sail no more,
For we'll find all we were promised, as we berth at Heaven's shore.
And the winds that filled our sails for us, will slowly die away,
As we dwell with those we missed so
much, forever and a day...Amen.

THE SOUL

Death has lost it's grip on me, for I know it's just a phase,
For the Lord has demonstrated that He has the power to raise.
It may well be, that part of me, will be buried underground,
But the souls of those who died in Christ,
we'll find are Heaven bound.

There comes a day for all of us to draw our final breath,
It's then our body and our soul, become detached by death,
The soul is lifted skywards on that our final day,
As the body that we don't require, is buried 'neath the clay.

The grave may serve it's purpose, I guess that's only fair,
As long as we remember, it's just our body resting there.
But if we've gave our heart to God, our spirit will survive,
And the soul that God has given us, is very much alive.

So death is just an obstacle, that each of us must climb,
A bridge that lies in front of us when we run out of time,
So come and do your very worst, I'm not prepared to hide,
For all of this will be worthwhile, when we
reach the other side...Amen.

THE GLORY

To God belongs the Glory, there's no-one quite like you,
My Faith I place in Jesus Christ, no other name will do.
I am but a servant, You're the one I choose to serve,
My Master who protects me, much more than I deserve.

The one who gives me guidance, through the challenges I face,
My comforter. my bread of life, my shield and resting place.
The one who sent His Son to Earth, to die that I might live,
The one who knows of all my sin, but is willing to forgive.

In you I find the strength I need, that wasn't there before,
In you I've everything I need, I couldn't ask for more.
You set me free, you rescued me, no longer am I bound,
And from above, you gave me love, that nowhere else is found.

You occupied this sinners heart, and gave my life a boost,
I thank God for that day and hour, that we were introduced.
Guide me both in word and deed, until my days are through,
Let every step I'm taking, bring me closer Lord to you...Amen.

THANKFUL

I am thankful in my times of need, there's a name to call upon,
A hand of comfort reaching out, to the anxious and forlorn.
A guiding light, in the darkest night, a flame to show the way,
A friend so dear, a listening ear, who hears us as we pray.

When we dwell in the deepest valley, we are lifted by His grace,
We are raised to mountain summit, to a less demanding place.
He's the comfort to the widow, when she is on her own,
And a Father to the orphans, so they are not alone.

He opens up His arms to us, when we think that no-one could,
He accepts us all as sinners, when we thought He never would.
We know that we're unworthy, and His love becomes our shame,
But yet He perseveres with us, and never seeks to blame.

He gave His very life for us, to remove our every stain,
Though every day, in every way, we let Him down again.
Yet I know He's standing with us, in everything we do,
Oh Jesus Christ, we'll never find, another friend like you...Amen.

THE OFFER

Sometimes we're made offers, that are too good to be true,
Being offered fame or fortune, by someone we never knew.
And greed can be our downfall, that makes us look a fool,
But all-in-all I know, there's one exception to the rule.

For I was once a sinner and in hell I knew I'd burn,
Yet Jesus gave forgiveness, asking nothing in return.
There isn't any obstacle, impossible to clear,
There isn't any enemy, in front of me I'll fear.

As long as I'm forgiven, I can take what comes along,
The blood of Jesus paid my bill, so how can I go wrong.
You can gamble with your offers, some
you'll win but most you'll lose,
But only Jesus makes an offer, you'd be foolish to refuse....Amen.

THE REQUEST

You only made the one request, that night you were betrayed,
To remember you as we drink the wine, and eat unleavened bread,
And after all you did for us, to set our hearts at rest,
How could we, in all honesty, refuse you this request.

The bread may be symbolic, of the body that was broken,
And we understand, for the blood you shed, This wine is just a token.
But each and every time, of this Communion I partake,
My eyes begin to water and my heart begins to break.

It's though you die a thousand deaths, your body wrecked by pain,
As we eat that bread and drink the wine, time and time again.
But you asked us to remember, and this we're proud to do.
To let you know we won't forget, and how much we love you.

So each time that we gather Lord, the first thing that we'll do,
Is raise the cup and eat the bread in remembrance of you.
We will do all that you asked of us, regardless of the pain,
As we hold firm to your promise, that your
coming back again....Amen.

THE BATTLE

When they drove that spear into your side,
they must have thought they'd won,
But the battle for the souls of Men, that day had just begun.
The cross became our battlefield, and we flew our standard High,
With Jesus unto victory, became our battle-cry.

We witnessed sights at Calvary, that caused us so much pain,
But our faith was soon rewarded, when you rose and walked again.
And everything we have and own, we owe it all to you,
We're strong of heart, We have the will, to see the battle though.

With Jesus there to lead us, we can vanquish any foe,
We will give our praise and glorify, in every place we go.
We will overcome all enemies, and scatter them like dust.
To God belongs the Glory, in Him we place our trust.

And peace will be restored as we put evil to the sword.
There'll be cries of celebration, when there's victory to the Lord.
And the sadness that was Calvary, will be forever swept away,
But we won't forget the sacrifice, that Jesus made that day....Amen.

SEASONS

Autumn pays it's visit, as the seasons make their trade,
And all the leaves of Summer, start to turn a different shade.
As the forests lose their foliage, we see such transformation,
And the squirrels once so busy, start to rest in hibernation.

But though things look so different, their really just the same,
The way we cannot change our God, when
He's called a different name.
Some may call Him Yahweh, others El Shaddai,
Some call Him El Elyon, Almighty God most High.

He's Alpha and Omega, The Lion and the Lamb,
Jehovah, Great Physician and the God of Abraham.
But no matter what we call Him, He loves us just the same,
And will not love us any less, if called by different name.

And when the summer comes around, the leaves will all return,
We'll bathe again in brightness in the warmness of the Sun.
Seasons may bring changes, that's the order of the game,
But the love of God is constant, and will
forever stay the same...Amen.

GONE HOME

We stood around that open grave, as they lowered the coffin down,
A friend who I'd grown up with, from the other side of town.
Andrew was a gentleman, who wouldn't hurt a fly,
The words I heard his widow speak, as a tear fell from her eye.

But had he come to know the Lord? was the question on my mind,
Though I didn't ask the question, for now was not the time.
Then umbrellas opened up, as the rain began to fall,
And we made our way towards our cars, for lunch in a little hall.

And while I waited in the queue for a welcome cup of tea,
I felt a hand upon my back, from the person next to me,
I turned to face the pastor, the one from at the grave,
It was then I found the courage, to ask was Andrew saved.

The pastor smiled and looked at me, his face was all aglow,
I led Andrew to the Lord, almost twenty years ago.
So although he was a sinner, He is cleansed by the blood of Christ
And we both knew, our friend Andrew,
now dwelt in Paradise....Amen.

THE SOLUTION

They tell us times are changing, but for better or for worse?
Are we edging to disaster, all because of Satan's curse?
The light that once shone brightly, has now become so dim,
For we've turned our backs on Jesus, and walked away from Him.

What happened to the Faith we had, it's nowhere to be found,
Bars and casinos open while there's churches closing down.
Do you think that God's abandoned us, at least that's how it feels,
For when one disaster happens, another follows on it's heels.

Have we really grown so ignorant, that we refuse to see,
The difference in this World today from how it used to be.
We need to demonstrate our love, we need to have respect,
We need to drop down on our knees, and ask our Saviour back.

Then maybe if we pray enough, the Lord will hear our plea,
He's the only hope that we have left, to change our destiny.
We need to take down barriers, if we are to survive,
For the God I love is in control, and Jesus is alive....Amen.

BE TRUE

To all those so-called pastors, and you know who you are,
Who feel the need for a private jet or expensive motorcar.
Cast your eyes to Jesus, and the example that He set,
Are you selective with your memory, what you remember or forget.

There may be those who's taken in, by the words you choose to use,
But I am one of the fortunate who hold some different views.
I believe that some are using God, in everything they do
To push their own agendas, regrettable but true.

We should all be serving Jesus, in every situation,
Without becoming victims to misguided exploitation.
If we are truly messengers that scatter all His seeds,
The Lord will be our portion and meet all of our needs.

Forget about celebrities, the wolf dressed in sheep's clothes,
I'm glad I am a Child of God, and was never one of those.
I may not have a fortune, but it's sufficient for my need,
My love of God takes precedence over gluttony and greed....Amen.

CHANGES

There are many things I'd like to change if I were in control,
To put an end to hunger, that would be my greatest goal,
I'd like to bring an end to war, yes, that would be my aim,
And expose those politicians, who are nothing like they claim.

I'd like to see democracy, replace the tyrants rule,
I'd love to see all children have the luxury of a school
I'd like to end child labour, so their burdens start to ease,
And free the masses from their chains, to worship as they please.

But above all this I'd like to see, the thing that we most lack,
I'd like to hear the trumpet, watch the clouds start rolling back.
I'd like to share the love of God with everyone I see.
I'd like to see all Nations live in perfect harmony.

But the Lord is soon returning, to put things back on track,
For Jesus gave His word to us, that soon He's coming back.
And I feel we really need Him, like we've never done before,
For this World of ours is in decay, and
cannot take much more.....Amen.

HE CAME

This world did not deserve you. but still with all you came,
Like a lamb into a lions den, to a place that knew no shame.
And surely Lord you must have known, the things that lay ahead,
The cross, the nails, that crown of thorns they placed upon your head.

You must have foreseen Calvary, and the pain to be endured,
For nothing from the Son of God could ever be obscured.
You must have known your Fathers plan, but yet you chose to stay,
Though you cried and prayed at Gethsemane,
please take this cup away.

But all along you must have knew, the cross was waiting there,
Of that suffering and indignity, you must have been aware.
But still you carried on my Lord, regardless of the cost,
And bled and died because of us, suspended on that cross.

But when you gave your life for us, the foundation had been laid,
For all our sin was washed away, by the sacrifice you made.
Was ever so much given, so undeservedly,
Than the life of one who cared so much, He gave unselfishly....Amen.

STRENGTH

Temperatures keeps rising because of how we live,
But when the strain becomes too much, something has to give.
Pressure so demanding, nerves begin to crack,
Until we face the final straw that breaks the camels back.

We find that we don't have the will there's not enough in store,
With all our strength exhausted, we still need a little more.
Yet comfort's just a prayer away, and we only need to ask.
The Lord is reaching out to us, to help us in our task.

His word is there to draw upon and I am living proof,
I'm empowered by the Grace of God and strengthened by His truth.
And while I wear the armour, that He has given me,
I have the strength to overcome my every enemy.

I have so much to thank Him for, how richly I've been blessed,
Through Him I emerge victorious from every battle faced.
I am stronger, I am wiser, when the Lord is on my side,
I can face each new tomorrow, with no necessity to hide....Amen

THE DECISION

When our head and hearts in conflict, decisions can be tough,
And no matter what advice we take, it's never quite enough.
We're trapped between two options, but
which one should we choose,
And it becomes more difficult when either way we lose.

But then again there comes the times, when head and heart agrees,
It's then we have the freedom, to decide just as we please.
So when I heard a voice inside, so softly call my name,
I couldn't quite decide if it was real or just a game.

But the more that I would listen, the more it all made sense,
I knew the Lord was calling me, and it wasn't just pretence.
My head was spinning wildly, and my heart felt like a stone,
But this was one decision that I had to make alone.

I knew I was a sinner, because of how I live,
But if I gave my life to Him, He was willing to forgive,
And since that day I've come to learn, that every word was true
That's why I gave my heart to Him, the proper thing to do.....Amen.

THE VINE

Each and every one of us are individual and unique,
But we share one thing in common, old or young, strong or weak.
For we have the same creator, we're a product of His Grace,
All created in His image, throughout time and throughout space.

And we need to tend our bodies, for we are fruit upon the vine,
For they become our Temple from a God who's so Divine,
He has moulded us and shaped us, we're essential to His plan,
We are pieces in His puzzle, every woman every man.

And as we wake each morning, to the dawn of another day,
We must spread His message far and wide, in each and every way.
For we are like the branches, that spread out from the root,
And the healthier the tree becomes, the greater is the fruit.

We must capture souls for Jesus, The Bible tells us so,
We must bring them to His garden, and tend them as they grow.
We must share the love we've found in Him, a love that's so extreme,
So we can make reality from what was once a dream.....Amen.

BURDENS

If there's one thing life has has taught me,
we will have our ups and downs,
Circumstances able, to turn laughter into frowns.
Yet frustration starts to fester, when we feel we're not to blame,
But we must try to face the good and bad
and treat them both the same.

So how are we to do that is the question you may ask,
When we're weighed down so heavily by the burden of our task.
The answers very simple, if you'll listen I can tell,
There's a pair of hands just waiting, that will serve you very well.

There's a Saviour out there calling, who will share the pain you feel,
Who will offer you His shoulder, and help the heartaches heal.
He's acquainted well with suffering, experienced in pain,
For He gave His life at Calvary, and would do it all again.

So the Sun will shine tomorrow, just you wait and see,
And the troubles you are facing, will become a memory.
You only have to call on Him, if the truth is to be told,
For His willing hands are capable of lightening any load…Amen.

THE ROUTE

If we set off on a journey, we always plan the route,
We choose our transport carefully, so the times we pick will suit,
We try to book our passage, by planning in advance,
And ensure that we are ready, leaving nothing down to chance.

We allow ourselves some extra time for hold-ups on the way,
Check that we have all we need, as we near departure day.
Then finally we're ready, all our plans have been worthwhile,
We can settle back, enjoy the trip, and even share a smile.

Well that's the way it is with life, that's gave to you and me,
We're granted time to plan ahead, for the life that is to be.
There's a journey we must undertake,
someday, somewhere, somehow.
If it's to be successful, we must start preparing now.

There won't be any motorway, airport, railway station,
And how we chose to live our lives, will decide our destination.
Two roads lie ahead of us, one to Glory, one to fire.
And only Jesus points the way, to the one that we desire....Amen.

PRISONERS

The air keeps getting thinner the higher that we climb,
The atmosphere grows colder when we leave the Earth behind,
So are we really captives, like prisoners in a cell,
Which to some may seem like Heaven, but to others feels like Hell.

Are the bodies we were given, just designed to keep us there,
For they depend on many things, like water, food and air.
When we think of all that we require, there's a never ending list,
But when I put my mind to it, there's more to life than this.

For our body's just a vessel, for the things we need to store,
But we possess a soul inside, that lives for evermore.
And when our Earthly days are done, we'll rise above the Sun,
And stand before the court of God, where He'll judge us one by one.

And that's where we will find ourselves, and that's where life begins,
So we must be sure before we go, we're forgiven of our sins.
The only way we'll find true peace, is to submit ourselves to Christ,
The one who went to Calvary, the one who paid the price...Amen.

PREPARE

If you think that life's eternal, you're in for quite a shock,
For time is quickly running out as the hands spin round the clock.
With every hour that passes, another night turns into day,
And all too soon we realize, that time has slipped away.

But don't let this reality check, cause you consternation,
For just like everything we do, it's about the preparation.
It's knowing we're not perfect, and will always make mistakes,
But asking for forgiveness, for all the time that takes,

It's knowing that we shy away from doing things we should,
It's knowing we're not perfect, but we did the best we could.
It's knowing if we ask the Lord, He's willing to forgive,
We fell short of His glory, but gave it all we had to give.

And I know He'll look upon us if we're honest and sincere,
And show mercy in His judgement, for the time we spent down here.
But we must start to earn His love, by the sweat upon our brow,
We need to clear the mist away, and start preparing now...Amen.

THAT DAY

There will come a day of deliverance, and not so long from now.
When the dead in Christ shall rise again, and every knee shall bow.
When the Nations come together and fall down at His feet,
And all the powers of darkness will be reeling from defeat.

Things will change forever when we hear that trumpet blast,
Death and pain will be no more, just memories from the past.
The blind will get to see again, they will have their sight restored,
As Satan's legions take to flight, when the Lion of Judah roared.

And Heaven will be our reward, for our faith in Him was strong
And at last the world will recognize, just who was right or wrong.
The day is drawing closer, soon the truth will be revealed,
The Son of God is coming back to take to battlefield,

And when the dust has settled, He will wear the Victors crown,
He promised He'd return again and He won't let us down.
That day is fast approaching, when we'll see again His face,
We only need to look around, the signs are all in place....Amen.

GOD IS LOVE

What's the definition of that thing we know as love,
If we want to know the answer, we must look to God above.
For Love is having patience, and Love is showing care,
Love is standing by someone to let them know you're there.

Love is undemanding, when mutually it's grown,
Love is placing someone's needs before your very own.
Love is selfless giving, like our blessings from above,
Or when you would sacrifice yourself, to save the one you love.

Love demands no payment, it's a gift completely free,
It's helping with the load I bear when the weights too much for me.
Loving is forgiveness, as we face another day,
Love is holding out a hand to dry the tears away,

So in answer to your question, I've done my very best,
And I pray, some day, you'll sample love, if that's become your quest.
But that's my definition, that's what I believe is true,
And all of this and so much more, I've found my Lord in you.....Amen.

REUNITED

You may well rise some morning, to the news we dread to hear,
That a faithful friend has been called home, and is no longer here.
But ask yourself the question, before the tears begin,
Did their heart belong to Jesus, were they forgiven of their sin?

Although there's pain in losing them we need to be aware,
For it may well make the tragedy much easier to bear.
If we know that now their resting and been granted their release,
In the arms of one they loved so much,
they've found their perfect peace.

So dry away those tears you shed before they reach the ground,
Be happy that their pain is gone in the new home they have found.
For someday we will meet again, in that truly wondrous place,
Where heartaches turn to victory, through
God's Amazing Grace....Amen.

THE FEELING

Of all the great achievement's that you will ever gain.
Or the highest level possible your likely to attain.
Of all the greatest victories that you will ever win,
Or outstanding bouts of pleasure that have brought the widest grin,

The joy of walking down the aisle, as a husband takes a bride,
The satisfaction that you feel, when on the winning side.
The exhilaration that you gain, when you're having so much fun.
The feeling of accomplishment, when you've got the hard job done.

All of these bring pleasure, but nowhere near as much,
As the moment you meet Jesus, and receive His loving touch.
Your world forever changes, as your given life anew,
As things that once were hidden, all come into view.

A transformation happens, that's so difficult to explain,
But I only know the life you had, you won't want back again.
You become a new creation, when you call on Jesus name,
And nothing else experienced, could ever feel the same....Amen.

EMERGENCE

It's my belief this world of ours is emerging from a drought,
As the seeds the Lord has planted, are beginning now to sprout.
We were dwelling in a wilderness, when
we thought He'd lost His fold,
But we see a new awakening as Revival's taking hold.

I believe that we lay dormant, just as silent as the dead,
But His churches start to fill again as His message starts to spread.
But a church is just a building, to accommodate a need,
We need to search the highways, there are souls out there to feed.

And soon we'll see the shoots appear if His seeds we start to sow,
Very soon we'll see the fruit appear as His church begins to grow.
And all will bathe in wondrous light, as He leads us from the dark,
When His message penetrates our Heart, as an arrow hits the mark.

Take a look around you, then tell me what you see,
This world is looking better now than how it used to be.
Souls are being saved again, and hearts are being won.
All praise to God Almighty, both the Father and the Son...Amen.

MY APOLOGY

I'm really very sorry for the way I make you cry,
My weaknesses take over Lord, no matter how I try.
My thoughts and deeds are good or bad, there is no compromise,
And I seem to open every prayer with "I apologise"

I'd like to make you proud of me, but I am not that strong,
And I recognise that every day, I seem to get things wrong.
Will today be any different? I'll have to wait and see,
Still I'm grateful that you've given me this opportunity.

But deep within this heart I know, I'll let you down again,
I can almost see the tears you'll cry, and how I'll cause you pain.
Yet you sacrificed your only Son to die that I might live,
I'm a sinner so unworthy of all the chances that you give.

But I guess there's no alternative, for what is done, is done.
The Sun begins to rise again, and another day's begun.
I trust I find the inner strength, so temptation I ignore.
And I live this day much better than the one that went before....Amen.

WHY?

I think about Gethsemane, the cross, the upper room
I think about the crown of thorns, the nails, the empty tomb.
I think of all the torment and how Lord Jesus bled,
Then I turn my thoughts to Mary, and the tears she must have shed.

I think about injustice and I fail to understand,
Why they inflicted so much cruelty upon a fellow man.
And the vision so upsets me that my tears begin to fall,
For it was only out of compassion, that He came to Earth at all.

The silhouetted picture of three crosses on a hill,
Instils in me such sadness and I guess it always will.
And even though He rose again, at the dawn on that third day,
It doesn't alter how I'm feeling, or make the sadness go away....Amen.

THE LIGHTHOUSE

Like the lighthouse in the harbour, sending out it's rays of light,
Like the candle burning brightly, in the darkness of the night,
Like the rainbow in the Heavens, just after we've had rain,
Like a formula for healing, that can take away all pain.

For we are all like vessels, and it's you who danger blocks.
In you we find security that keeps us off the rocks,
And when we walk in darkness, then the Lord becomes our sight,
When we're dwelling in the shadows, then
it's you who spreads His light.

Your the reassurance when the storms of life appear,
The rainbow in the heavens let's us know your always near.
And your the hand of healing that can take away the pain,
Your touch contains the power to bring us back to health again.

All in all your wonderful, in you I place my trust,
You demonstrate in many ways, how much you care for us.
Your the Father, we your children, you have granted life anew,
Your the love transcending others, and we all depend on you...Amen

THE RANSOM

What if Christ my Saviour had never come to Earth,
And there was no crucifixion and there was no Virgin Birth,
And we never had a teacher, to tell us what would pass,
And we carry all our sin with us 'til we breathe our very last,

If we never got to hear the wondrous news He had to tell,
Would every single one of us, spend eternity in Hell.
Would He never heal the leper, the sightless and the lame,
Would Faith be non-existent, and our lives not be the same.

This picture that I'm painting, is not a pretty one,
But this was all avoided when a Father sent His Son.
We got to hear His lessons and the message that He brought,
He promised that the Life ahead is much better than we thought.

But best of all He gave us hope, when there was just dismay,
When He shed His blood at Calvary to wash our sin away.
And this world was paid a ransom, worth more than any gem,
When a baby was delivered in a place called Bethlehem...Amen.

PROTECTED

If we've gave our hearts to Jesus, we're protected by His Grace,
But never underestimate the challenges we face.
For Satan can be cunning, interfering with our minds,
And will do his best exploiting any weaknesses he finds.

But I've been taught a lesson, that I never will forget,
That Satan just attacks the ones that he regards a threat.
So if I should feel his presence, I'll be preparing for the fight,
If he's took the time to challenge me, I'm doing something right.

There's a barrier surrounding me, and the Lord has placed it there,
That the devil cannot penetrate, I know he wouldn't dare,
For defeat can taste so bitter, And he's tasted it before,
And just a fool would return again, and get to taste some more.

So we are never vulnerable we're protected by the Lamb,
The blood of Jesus washes us, and that's what keeps us calm.
Take your stand for Jesus, keep His standard flying high,
So Satan has no option, but to keep on passing by....Amen.

CONFLICT

If I walk away from conflict, it doesn't mean that I'm a coward,
I'm just avoiding confrontation, even though it's very hard.
If I try to hold my silence, when there's something to be said,
These were lessons taught by Jesus, that I know must be obeyed.

When I place my trust in others, but they often disappoint,
When a fire inside me rages and approaches boiling point.
If I'm seeking retribution, when a rival made me cry,
I must follow God's instruction, it's the code I must live by.

No-one said it would be easy. And at times I may well slip,
In the past there's been occasions where I can't control my lip.
But each day I'm trying harder, to be the best that I can be,
And through the precious blood of Jesus
I know that He's forgiven me.

But I know I haven't licence, to sin just as I please,
And I often say I'm sorry when my temper starts to ease.
But I'm glad there is a Saviour, one that I have found at last,
For I'm now a better person, than I was in the past…Amen.

DIRECTION

If you haven't yet found Jesus, you must dwell among the blind,
With a heart as cold and empty, as the tomb He left behind.
If you claim you cannot find Him, your not searching very much
For His love is so apparent, in everything I see and touch,

His voice is clear and audible. it's carried on the breeze,
His grace is found in great amounts, His mercy grants me ease.
His comfort is my resting place, His caring my release,
In His arms I find my sanctuary, His sacrifice my peace.

I can feel Him all around me, watching over me with care,
And when I correspond with Him, I know He's always there.
He provides the light that guides my path, no matter where I go,
His Angels guard my every step, like nothing else I know.

So it's difficult to understand why you don't feel Him too,
But maybe soon you will believe when He stands in open view,
For He left us with a promise, that He's coming back again.
To rid this world of evil, and His Kingdom to regain...Amen.

OFFENDED

Some things really bother me, and penetrate my skin,
Most of these symbolic of the days we're living in,
When I hear the word "offended" how it really gets to me,
When they use it as a weapon aimed at those who disagree.

Things were never quite so bad, away back in the day,
When, If we became offended, we would simply walk away,
If someone didn't want to hear, It hardly made the news,
But now it's just a barrier, to silence others views,

So how are you offended, when the words we share are true?
How can someone cause offence when He gave His life for you?
What is so offensive that you cannot bear to hear?
Is the message of the scriptures so offensive to your ear?

Would you rather we stayed silent, to things you never knew,
Than share the joy we've found in Christ, that you may find it too?
There will come a day you'll thank us, for all we had to say,
And I wonder how "offended" you'll be feeling on that day....Amen.

PAID

When I stand before the Father, will He ask me to depart,
Or will He see the flame that burns for Jesus in my heart.
Will He know that when I see the cross, I can't but shed a tear,
Will He open up the Book of Life, and see my name appear.

Though I may not have a lot to give, His love for me endures,
So everything I have and own, please take it Lord, it's yours.
I came into this world with nothing, and I'll leave it just the same,
And every blessing I received, through the will of God it came.

I humbly bow before you Lord, unworthy and with shame,
For my sins I am accountable, there's no-one else to blame.
You let me make decisions when you gave the gift of choice,
And I'm sorry for the times I did not listen to your voice.

So my future's at your mercy, my fate lies in your hand,
Whatever your decision is, I will try to understand.
But the best defence I offer, and my one and only plea,
Is the sacrifice that Jesus made, and the blood of Calvary.....Amen.

ENSLAVED

If you've become a slave to your addictions,
like a hostage to a bottle or a pill,
There's a hand out there to help you overcome them,
who can turn your highest mountain to a hill.
He will give you strength and take away temptation,
and grant you all the will-power that you lack,
When, for every forward step you think you're
taking, in reality you've taken two steps back.

If you've lots of friends when there's money in your
pockets, but when penniless a friend cannot be found,
There is one prepared to be a true companion, who
regardless will still raise you off the ground.
Or if others try to judge you by appearance, and
maybe look at you in sheer disgust,
He'll accept you just however you approach Him, if
you have the faith to place in Him your trust.

You'll find that contrary to what your thinking,
there's still someone who loves you after all,
If you'll open up your heart and let Him enter, for
He's listening and waiting for your call.
There is no-one who's beyond the love of Jesus,
so never think that you have gone too far,
You only need to ask for His forgiveness, and I know
He'll take you just the way you are…Amen.

MY ALL

Your word is like the nectar, that's collected by the bee,
Your love for me like honey, just as sweet as it can be.
Your Grace is like a flower, transformed from just a seed,
Your presence is essential, for it's all I'll ever need.

Your mercy never ending, is the rock that I cling to,
Your guidance is the thing required, in all I say and do.
Your promises, the bandages, that help my wounds to heal,
Your forgiveness of this sinner is the happiness I feel.

You give me strength to rise above the challenges I meet,
You help me snatch a victory, when I'm staring at defeat.
Your blessings are my food and drink, by which I am sustained.
The Son you gave has paid the bill, For a heart so badly stained,

Your hands contain the power for the roughest seas to calm.
My very life I owe to you, like the Son of Abraham.
I offer all I have to you, Until for me you send,
I pray that you'll abide with me, stay with me to the end…Amen.

SOMETIMES

Sometimes it felt I was living in denial
There were times I felt like throwing in the towel.
But when my faith was on the wane, Jesus touched me once again,
It was His love for me that brought me through the trial.

When worries made my heart sink like a stone,
When I thought I'd have to face them on my own.
Until Jesus intervened, became the staff on which I leaned,
And ensured I never carried them alone.

When I needed help but no-one seemed to care,
When the pain I felt became too much to bear.
He felt my isolation, gave me strength and consolation,
When I needed Him, I'm sure that He was there.

I'm so grateful for the lessons He has taught.
He has helped me in the battles I have fought,
Time and time again, He's bound my wounds and bore my pain,
And through His precious blood, my sin has all been bought…Amen.

HE LEADS

I think of all the things you said, your words
keep swimming round my head,
If only I could be much more like you.
In a world condemned to doubt and strife,
where sin is just a way of life,
You came to teach us things we never knew.

To love the meek, to turn the cheek, to pray
for strength when I grow weak,
To offer up a hand to those in need.
To conquer fraud, to worship God, to lean on Him each road we trod,
And never let our lives be ruled by greed.

But even after all this time, our world is still immersed in crime,
So your words are still as relevant today.
But you wasted tears, on broken ears, even after all these years,
Despite the wisdom of the things you had to say.

Yet when things get flawed, I find it odd, the
one we seek is the Son of God,
And Jesus is the name we call upon,
For He's always there, to hear each prayer,
with a love that is beyond compare,
Through the darkest night He'll lead us to the dawn..Amen.

OUR ONLY HOPE

If you saw the world through my eyes, how different things would be,
You'd understand the way I feel and the hopelessness I see,
You'd see the unborn babies being torn from Mother's womb,
You'd see the homeless on the streets, so desperate for a room,

Perhaps the starving children, in a world that doesn't care,
Then maybe you'd be grateful, that your here instead of there,
You'd see the pointless killing, and wonder what it's for,
You'd see curse of poverty, when there's millions spent on war,

You'd see how we've accepted Sin and forgotten how to cry
How the rich enjoy their banquets, while those with nothing die.
How perpetrators benefit, and the victim doesn't count.
And the drugs that kill our Children, now exist in great amount.

And then you ask me earnestly, why my Faith in God is sound,
When the Lords the only chance we have. of turning things around.
But when I come to think of it. perhaps we've gone too far.
We've reached the point of no return,
because of what we are...Amen.

BELIEF

I believe the Lord is watching, the persecution Christians face,
I believe His heart is breaking as the tears stream down His face,
But I also think He's angry, when He sees their suffering,
All because they've gave allegiance to an everlasting King.

I believe this world's a darker place, forever growing dim,
And It seems too many martyrs have laid down their lives for Him.
But I believe that retribution day is waiting just ahead,
When the price for all corruption will have to be repaid.

I believe the great imposters, very soon will be exposed,
I feel sorry for the followers who've been misled by all of those.
Who failed to follow Jesus, and were brainwashed and deceived?
If only they had listened, if only they'd believed.

But they chose to follow charlatans, with money as their goal,
Now they've missed out on Eternity, and forfeited their soul,
For you should have followed Jesus, He's the only path to take,
But when you failed to read the Bible, that
became your worst mistake.... Amen.

THE ANSWERS

The greatest minds have tried their best, but puzzles yet remain,
There will always be, some mystery, that science can't explain.
We've invented some solutions, so the answers fit the bill,
But we've only scratched the surface and I guess we always will.

It's beyond our comprehension, like a code we'll never crack,
So sometimes we must trust in God for the answers that we lack.
We need to show a little faith, or otherwise we're bound,
For its only when we look to Him, the answers will be found.

He set the wheels in motion, when He created all the Earth,
And inquisitiveness has haunted us, since Man was given birth.
We possess a thirst for knowledge, that is hard to satisfy,
Yet there's many things we can't explain no matter how we try.

Every question has an answer, but let's just be content,
For when He feels the time is right, the answers will be sent.
He has reasons for His actions, that no man understands,
But all will be revealed some day, when
we're resting in His hands.... Amen.

THE VERDICT

We can never say with confidence, we've earned our place above,
Or never say with certainty; we've gained our Saviours' love.
For although the road we walk upon is paved with good intention,
Too easily we forget our sins, or are too ashamed to mention,

But when we stand before His throne, all will be revealed,
Our lives become an open book, where nothing is concealed.
And I shake in trepidation at how I'll handle that ordeal,
When my fate will rest in Jesus' hands, no adjournment or appeal.

But we can't escape our judgement, it lies ahead of us,
We must place our trust in Jesus Christ, that His verdict will be just.
Perhaps you've never given thought to how you'll act that day,
Or perhaps to leave it down to luck for what you'll do or say,

But the candle's burning rapidly as the days so quickly pass,
And no-one knows the day or hour that will become their last.
So whatever time we're granted we should use it to prepare,
For our time will come to take the stand, and
judgement's waiting there...Amen.

TURN TO HIM

Forever on the losing side, and yet to taste success,
A broken man, an also ran, your life a total mess.
Destined for a bridesmaid but never quite the bride,
The one whose friends would never pick,
if they should choose the side.

The one who always gets the blame, when fingers point at you,
There are some prepared to call you friend,
but they number just a few.
The black sheep of the family, a weed but not a flower,
The one whose friends don't take the time to ask you how you are.

But when you've reached rock bottom, and your life's an empty cup,
There's one direction you can go, and that is pointing up.
You need to wipe the dust away, and those tears will soon depart,
You need the love of one who's there, to mend a broken heart,

You need to call on Jesus, He's waiting to be found,
He's the only one that's capable, of turning lives around.
Misery turns to happiness, and boredom turns to fun,
You'll be thankful that you turned to Him, when
your new life has begun...Amen.

CONTENT

With the Sun on the rise, I will open my eyes,
to the dawn of a beautiful day,
And I'll kneel by my bed, as I lower my head,
and engage with the Lord as I pray.
It's His guidance I seek, and He'll hear as I speak,
and I trust He will grant my request,
To protect me this day, and guard come what
may, how beautifully I have been blessed.

And as day turns to night, as we're losing the
light, I will offer my thanks once again,
That the day that I spent, and wherever I went,
I witnessed no sorrow nor pain.
That the Lord that I served, gave me more than
deserved, I'm unworthy but yet He shows care,
But I hope He can see, I'm the best I can be,
even though of my sin He's aware.

So I'll climb into bed, after all I have said,
and peacefully drift off to sleep,
Consoled by His love, as He watches above,
like a shepherd takes care of his sheep.
And perhaps it may be, that my dreams carry
me, to a place far away as the Sun,
Yet if I never rose, and my eyes remain closed, I'd still
know that His will has been done.... Amen.

CHANGE

Optimism tells us that where there's life there's hope,
People are adaptable, and that's what makes them cope.
But sometimes change is difficult, if we're set in our ways,
We try to disregard our wrongs, but their memory always stays.

But forgiveness is a virtue, that we can all attain,
For the Lord can wipe the blackboard clean, so we can start again.
He can take away the guilt we feel, like no-one else I know,
He can take the very blackest heart and make it white as snow.

He'll take away your heavy load and heal the scars you bear,
He'll bind your wounds and bear your pain, as though it wasn't there.
You only need to come to Him, He won't turn you away,
He'll welcome you with open arms and you can change today.

No other gift in all the world can be bought at any price,
Than the gift of true forgiveness, that was bought by Jesus Christ.
So join the ranks of those He's saved, get right with God this time,
So the hills that lie in front of you are easier to climb.... Amen.

IT'S TIME

If you call yourself a Child of God, will you step up to the mark,
And spread His message far and wide, for the times we face are stark,
We can see the consequences as this World of ours grows dim,
But what else can we all expect, when we turn our backs to Him.

Loyalty is a two-way street, that we must give to gain,
And because we've walked away from God,
this worlds consumed by pain.
But the God I knows forgiving and He has the power to mend,
But if this is to happen, then our silence has to end.

For only when we show remorse, will the tides begin to turn,
And all will see, His majesty, if we ask Him to return.
So if we want to get things back to how they used to be,
We need to send our Praise to God for worship is the key.

It's how we raise our Children, that will make them who they are,
And we should hang our heads in shame at the job we've done so far.
For only when we turn to God, will His promises He'll keep.
And He'll lift us from this hole we've dug,
before it gets too deep...Amen.

OUR CHURCH

The God we serves amazing, He's a truly wondrous friend,
I'm ecstatic He directed us to the church that we attend.
We can think of nothing better or where else we'd rather be,
Than the church to where He led us, where we're all one family.

We may not run to hundreds, but our Faith in Him's sincere,
It's so good to know He watches us; we can feel Him standing near.
From the moment that we entered. it was very clear to see
We were welcomed to the family, just the way a church should be.

We all pull in one direction, and our love for Him's the same.
For everything we say and do, we do in Jesus' name
We've a caring loving Saviour and the words He spoke were true,
That where two or three are gathered, I
am in the midst of you.... Amen

THEY WATCHED

Forgiveness unconditional, a love without a price,
By the Son of God who paid our debt, His life the sacrifice.
Yet they gathered not to thank Him, but instead to watch Him die,
As their welcomes of Hosanna turned to chants of crucify.

They watched them nail Him to that cross, and hoist it in the air,
Yet did not realize it was their sin that held Him there.
They watched the Roman soldiers, as they mocked Him and abused,
When the sign they placed above His head,
proclaimed Him King of Jews.

They saw that crown of thorns, the soldiers placed upon His head,
They saw the wounds inflicted, yet still mocked Him as He bled.
And they must have heard Him mutter, as the pain inside Him grew,
Please forgive them Father for they know not what they do.

And then I think of Mary and the tears she must have cried,
As He muttered It Is Finished, with the spear that pierced His side,
And how they took His broken body, all that anguish, hurt and pain,
Not suspecting that in three days' time, He'd
walk the Earth again.... Amen

FOR THOSE I LOVE

I spare a thought for those I love, the ones I hold so dear,
And pray if I shout loud enough, eventually they'll hear,
But I need your help Lord Jesus, to get my message through,
So when I find I'm lost for words, that's when I turn to you.

If you would grant this wish of mine, then I would ask no more,
If only you'd instruct me how to lead them to Your door.
And help to make them realize, that all I say is true,
But my words cannot convince them Lord, that's why I turn to You.

I pray as each day passes, they will open up their hearts,
Each and every one, before another soul departs.
So we can be united when our days on earth are through,
But I can't do it on my own, that's why I turn to you.

I know your Father has a plan, from beginning to the end,
If only they'd submit to Him, this broken heart would mend.
Then I'd know some day I'd meet again with all the friends I knew,
You're the Saviour who can soften hearts,
and I depend on you.... Amen.

UNDERSTANDING

When troubles just keep rolling in like breakers on the shore,
When problems start to weigh you down 'til you can take no more,
If you're feeling isolated or embarrassed by your plight,
There's a Saviour you can turn to, who'll make everything alright.

If the world that you inhabit is a dark and lonely place,
When friends are well outnumbered by the enemies you face
If there's none prepared to listen or much less understand,
The Lord is still there waiting and holding out His hand.

If you waken up each morning with another sense of dread,
When hopelessness presents itself for the day that lies ahead.
When each horizons darker and the future's only bleak,
Jesus holds the answers if only you would seek.

He grants rest to the weary, bring hope where there is none,
He'll lift your burdens, break your chains
when your life with Him's begun.
The skies above grow brighter when He's walking by your side,
And a smile can take the place of all those tears you tried to hide.

You only have to call his name, no other words required,
You'll find that He's the missing piece that you've so long desired.
Problems still present themselves, but on a different scale,
When you've found a friend in Jesus Christ,
who's love will never fail...Amen

TOTALLY

When we submit our lives to Jesus, it's in differing amounts,
But it's not about the time we give, it's
what's in our hearts that counts.
For our behaviour's truly indicate, if we're living in denial,
So what would be the verdict, if your Faith was put on trial?

Have you placed your total trust in Him,
is the love you give Him true?
Does the name of Jesus motivate, like no other name can do?
Before you go to bed each night, do you speak with Him in prayer?
Would your life begin to crumble, if you found He wasn't there?

When you see the cross of Calvary, do your emotions start to show,
When you see His broken body, do your tears begin to flow?
Do you thank Him for each day He grants,
and the Sun upon your face?
Are you happy He's forgiven you by the beauty of His Grace?

For these become the measures, when our time on Earth is through,
And not because of what we say or anything we do.
Jesus paid for all our sin, His blood has set us free,
And if we only trust in Him, the rest comes naturally......Amen.

THE STORY

This is the book, enriched by the truth, that tells a wondrous story,
Of Jesus Christ, and His sinless life, to Him belongs the glory.
This is the hill, the cross of wood, that took His life away,
And this the tomb, now an empty room,
that proves He is living today.

This is the voice, that helps me rejoice, that you'll often hear as I raise
I will worship the Son, for my true life begun,
so worthy is He of my praise.
This is the man, both the Lion and the Lamb,
the Life, and the Truth and the Way,
And this is the blood, that He shed for me, to carry my sins all away.

These are the hands, that await His commands, dutiful, loyal and true,
It's His strength that I seek, for I sometimes get
weak, but He knows it's the best I can do.
And this is the heart, of which He is part, so easily subject to pain,
Before Jesus I knew, it was broken in two,
but He put it together again.

And these are the ears, that allowed me to hear,
that day when He called out my name,
How my life that day changed, how He rearranged,
and my life was never the same.
And these are the eyes that one day will see, that
wonderful mansion He's promised to me,
Only love now remains, since He's broken my chains,
and the blood that He shed set me free......Amen.

WAITING

The time I feel is very fast approaching, for we've
broken up this world and left it scarred,
From the paradise that God above created,
to what I see today is very hard.
Destruction seems to have reached another
level, as into evils trap we all succumb,
And only Jesus has the power to fix it, so I urge
you Jesus when you're ready, come.

You taught us by example when we listened, should
we follow you then you would pave the way
But the goodness just went slipping through our
fingers, and our carelessness has let it slip away.
Pestilence and war has taken over, until the
skies above the battlefield are black
So please listen to this heartfelt plea I send you, we
need you so much Jesus, please come back.

You told us that your work on Earth was finished,
but promised us that you'd return again,
So You're the only thing that's left for me to cling too,
in this world so full of sorrow, grief and pain.
And though it grieves my heart to see the mass
destruction, I won't stand idly by and watch it burn,
So I'm counting down the days and hours and minutes,
as I'm eagerly awaiting your return.... Amen

THE GATHERING

From every walk of life they must have gathered,
mothers and the children that they brung,
There were those who's ages couldn't be determined,
the old, the middle aged and then the young.
There were also those who dressed up very formal, while
the young preferred a Tee shirt and some jeans,
There were those who had to save up for their tickets,
even though the cost was way beyond their means.

From this description you could be forgiven, if you
thought that they had come to watch a show.
A Movie or a concert by a Pop star, or to
listen to some celebrity we know.
But the audience was just made up of Christians, and
those who'd asked a friend to come along,
They were there to learn about the life of Jesus. and
to give their praise and worship in a song.

Every denomination was represented, the
church that you attended didn't count,
Affiliation would not be considered, that wasn't
what this gathering was about.
You didn't know the person sat beside you, but
divisions were all left outside the door
We only shared a common love for Jesus,
that's what Christianity is for.

And the unity we sensed was so electric, it was
felt by all of those that filled the hall,
Catholic, Pentecostal, Jew or Baptist, or those
who didn't have a church at all.
So if we can spend an hour or two together,
where differences can all be set aside,
Then we only need the will to live together, and
maybe we can start to turn the tide.... Amen

SELFISHNESS

The things that come for free we take for granted,
with no consideration come what may,
We grumble at the slightest inconvenience,
whenever things refuse to go our way.
We seldom spare a thought for others feelings, we're
just concerned with putting ourselves first,
But one day very soon the change is coming,
and shortly we will see the bubble burst.

For the Bible tells us we should love our neighbour,
the most important commandment of them all,
And that's the benchmark we should be attaining, for
it determines whether we should rise or fall.
We need to show a little more compassion, and
be considerate in all we say and do,
We need to be forgiving in our nature, the
way that Jesus Christ's forgiven you.

We need to be the one our friends can turn to, and
assist them in the troubles that they face,
Then surely if we take the time to do this, this
world or ours will be a better place.
The lives we live are not a competition, so these
are things we need to rise above,
Then the barriers that divide us can be dismantled, and
selfishness can be replaced by love.... Amen.

HUNGER

As I wipe away the tears at what I'm watching, I'm
convinced this world's controlled by only greed,
For it breaks my heart to watch the Children suffer,
when I know that there's sufficient food to feed.
And if you've ever felt the pangs of hunger, you'll
know it's not a simple game we play,
But maybe you are too ashamed to watch them,
though that doesn't make the problem go away.

This heart of mine is bleeding for the victims, as I
watch them all reduced to skin and bone,
So to all of those who have the means to end it, would
you help if they were Children of your own?
Do you believe that your success is gauged by profits,
are you content to watch them slowly die?
Do you consider profiteering over Children,
when they haven't got the energy to cry?

But the only shred of comfort that I cling to, is by
knowing very soon there'll come a day,
For the King of Kings and Lord of Lords is coming,
so that pain and hunger may be swept away.
So when the Nations all bow down before Him,
can they justify the actions that they took,
For the profits that they made will count for nothing, if they
find their names are missing from His book.... Amen.

FOR

For every drop of rain that falls from Heaven,
another flower on Earth begins to grow,
And for every soul who leaves this world forgiven,
another star in Heaven starts to glow.
For every heart that searches for forgiveness,
Jesus Christ will come and point the way,
And for every sin that ever was committed, the
blood of Jesus paid for on that day.

For every hill we climb there is a valley, and every
thought we're thinking God will know,
And in Heaven there are many, many mansions,
if not the case He would have told us so.
For every storm that gathers He's the shelter, for
every hardened heart He is the cure,
For laying down the path that we are taking and
guarding us from everything impure.

For every ray of sunshine that He sends us, for
the harvest that we gather from the field,
For protecting us whenever danger threatens, for the
knowledge that His love will be our shield.
So in every situation I encounter, I'm forgiven,
I'm protected, I'm sustained,
And even though the sins I have are countless, despite
them all His love for Me's remained.... Amen

HIS RETURN

What will I be doing, and I wonder where I'll be,
When the clouds above me open up and Jesus Christ I see,
Will I shield my eyes to guard them, as I look upon His face?
Will my body start to tremble at the power of His Grace?

Though none of us have knowledge of the time, the place, the date.
I only know He's coming, and we won't have long to wait.
There'll be cries of celebration when we see Him drawing near,
Some will kneel to worship Him, while others cower in fear.

Will He bring with Him His armies, a mighty Angel host?
Will we see in Him the Trinity, Father, Son and Holy Ghost.
Will we hear the battle raging, will the battlefield be stained,
When evil is defeated, and His Kingdom is regained.

And when the dust has settled, will we feel His loving touch,
As He leads us all to Heaven and the ones we miss so much.
Will we stand in pure amazement and in unison applaud?
As we listen to the Angels sing, by the Citadel of God....Amen.

SHOUT

Misinterpretation is a danger, if we decide to hide our faith away,
For too long we've been hiding in the shadows, so
our message never sees the light of day.
It's time to leave the comfort of our churches, and
speed across the nations like a storm,
To demonstrate the love we hold for Jesus and
dispel the myth our faith is just luke warm.

For how can we bring others to His Kingdom, when
we're not prepared to delve into the dirt,
For that's where we will find the souls who need Him,
down there among the hopeless and the hurt.
The time has come when we must raise our voices,
for the time of being silent's in the past
It's time to leave the trenches we are digging,
it's time to nail our colours to the mast.

Then maybe we can gain the world's attention, as
at last they start to recognize our cause,
But only if we shout instead of whisper, and
really start to make a lot of noise.
For the God we serve is worthy of our voices, we
need some sturdy hearts and steady nerves,
For when we sing our praises for His Glory, He'll start
to gain the respect that He deserves.... Amen.

NEVER

Never before did I feel such strong emotions,
or experience a feeling such as this,
Never before did I understand the meaning, of
what you never had you never miss.
Until that day I gave my heart to Jesus, and
all my worry seemed to disappear,
So now I've come to understand completely, and
the meaning of those words are crystal clear.

For before I came to take Him as my Saviour,
the need of Him was never on my list,
But now I realise how much He loves me, if I
should ever lose Him, He'd be missed.
My love for Him could not be any stronger, so
much so that words cannot define,
For the one who used His body as my ransom, to
pay the price for the sin that all was mine.

So if you've yet to find the love He offers, or you
haven't felt the forgiveness of His Grace,
Then you'll understand the day that you accept Him,
it's an experience that nothing can replace.
So when you hear the voice of Jesus calling,
accept His hand and greet it with a kiss,
For after all there's truth in what their saying, that
what you never had you never miss.... Amen.

THE JOURNEY

Have you ever pondered on the life that's coming,
and that place that Jesus taught us lies ahead?
Have you given any thought to what He taught us, or
been too wrapped up in the present day instead?
Does disappointment always seem to haunt you,
when nothing turns out quite the way it seems
Does your pillow provide your only source of comfort,
and the best escape you have is in your dreams?

For the final breath we draw is not the ending,
in terms of contradiction it's the start,
For the souls we have I know will go on living,
long after there's no beating from our heart.
So when we reach our final destination, will
you find yourself in a paradise sublime,
Will you be carried by His Grace and gain His favour,
for eternity you knows a long, long time.

To a place where you can dwell among the Angels,
a place where none will witness any tears,
With songs of praise just waiting there to greet you,
that I know will be sweet music to your ears.
Where all the sights and sounds that you encounter,
bear no resemblance to the world you left below,
And the splendour of a paradise will lead you to
where refreshing streams of crystal waters flow,

All of this is yours just for the taking, you only
need to ask, and you'll receive,
And in return the only restitution, He requires
you demonstrate that you believe.
And when your Earthly body you abandon, when your
called to come on that your Judgement day.
If you look towards the Heavens while you journey,
Jesus you will find will point the way.... Amen

TOMORROW

Should the skies fall down tomorrow would I worry,
should the air that I rely on disappear,
Should the earth beneath my feet begin to crumble,
it really wouldn't cause me any fear.
For I've placed my faith and trust in my Lord Jesus,
and I know that He's the keeper of my soul,
So no matter what this world can bring upon me,
I know the God I serve is in control.

And if he chose to end this world tomorrow, I'd
be grateful for the time He's given me.
I wouldn't dare to question His decision, for
who are you and I to disagree?
I would humbly take my stand before my maker,
and ponder on the time that I have used,
And I'd pray as He delivers up His Judgement, that
He would not find one second was abused.

But the promise that He gave to us is holding, as
we watch the rainbow forming in the sky,
And it won't be God who moves His hand against us,
This world we share's condemned by you and I.
The little piece of Heaven that He gave us, the
beauty that was created by His hand,
We have bled it dry of all of its resources, so we
can't expect Him now to understand.

We have taken all the roses from His garden,
turned a paradise into a battlefield,
And by our greed we've pillaged and exploited,
until the Earth has nothing left to yield.
So we can't deny that God has shown us mercy,
He's pardoned us for a litany of crime,
But I know the Lord is coming for His Kingdom, and
quickly we are running out of time!...... Amen.

MY PROVIDER

My pockets may be empty, and I've nothing in the bank,
But I am rich in other ways, and it's God I have to thank.
His love for me is everything, He keeps me in His care,
No matter if I'm a pauper or a multi- millionaire.

There's no hierarchy in Heaven, status doesn't count,
It's what you hold within your heart, and not in your account.
The wealth I have is deep inside, where none can steal away,
My balance still increases, each and every time I pray.

Interest rates don't bother me, my currency is love,
My cup keeps overflowing, with my blessings from above.
I may not wear designer clothes, or holiday abroad,
Yet I have everything I need, as long as I have God.

From the roof where I take cover to the food I have inside.
The air I need to stay alive, I know that He'll provide.
My fortune lies in Heaven, in that place He's promised me,
For I have Jesus as my broker and His word my guarantee......Amen

DECISIONS

Life demands that we must make our choices,
influenced by many different voices,
Some we might regret, and others wish we could forget,
But when we get them right, our heart rejoices.

There are decisions where we exercise great care,
like what we eat or we decide to wear,
But if you listen to me please, there's more important ones than these,
And one that I believe it's right to share.

Do you believe in all the things that Jesus told, have
you planned for what the future may well hold?
For we owe Him everything, does your heart belong to Him,
Will you be with Him where streets are paved with gold.

So, consider this decision that you make, it's
the most important you will ever take,
There's a gate in front of you, that just the Lord can bring you through,
You'll be accepted when you ask in Jesus sake.... Amen.

GODS WORD

Clear your mind when studying the Bible,
for total concentration is the key,
For a river only flows in one direction as it
slowly winds its way towards the sea.
We can never concentrate if we're distracted,
or focus if our mind is split in two,
You must open up your heart to what your reading,
if you want God's truth to be revealed to you.

There is wisdom in abundance in its pages,
Knowledge there just waiting to be found,
All dictated by our Alpha and Omega and contained
within the word He handed down.
The word of God is a fountain overflowing, and it
describes the many gifts He has to give.
And if your heart is open to its message, its
truth transforms the very way we live.

It reveals to us the answer to Life's purpose, it
tells how we need rescue from our sin,
Step by step we learn about Salvation, and somehow
through it's chapters we're drawn in.
There is power to be found when we consider,
that every word we're reading's really true,
And each and every time I read a passage; I
never fail to discover something new.

But like I said way back at the beginning, clear
all other thoughts out of your mind,
And the Grace of God will then descend upon you,
all the answers you are looking for, you'll find.
It's the only source we truly can depend on, where
so many of Life's secrets are unmasked,
It will shine a light where there was only darkness and
answer every question you have asked......Amen.

THE SEARCH

You could spend a lifetime looking for what's missing,
that elusive thing that makes a life complete,
You could travel far and wide and never find
it, with every effort ending in defeat.
And with every passing hour you grow more weary,
and you wonder will your journey never cease,
But still you carry on with determination, not
content until you find that missing piece.

But every path you've taken ends up fruitless.
even when you've tried your very best,
But your stubbornness will always keep you searching,
you won't give in til you complete your quest.
So the Sun begins to rise on the horizon, your
opportunity to take another shot,
To try to find the joy you see in others, what
is it they have got that you have not?

Maybe you've been searching in wrong places, for
its only in the mind that peace is found,
And the envy that you feel for all the others, is because
they've lost the chains that had them bound.
So the only thing that ever really matters, the
thing to fill that emptiness you feel,
Is the knowledge that your heart belongs to Jesus, and
then your scars can really start to heal...Amen

WHO

The one who's always there to lend a shoulder,
the one who's ever there to dry your tears,
The one who's always offered their protection, who has
stood with you throughout those childhood years.
The one who'd always wait until you're ready,
despite the many hours the waiting took,
Who remained with you when others all departed, that
you knew was there and didn't have to look?

The one with whom you got to share your secrets,
confident that they would never tell,
The one who understood when others didn't and
was always there to lift you when you fell.
The one who brought you through your greatest sorrow,
who never failed to help the heartaches mend,
Who defended you when others spoke against
you, for that's the definition of a friend?

There's only one that ticks all of these boxes,
for only one could ever be so true,
The one who never walks away and leaves you,
the one who gave His very life for you.
We will forfeit many friendships in our life time,
for many of them simply come and go,
But if you have a friend and call Him Jesus, He's the
greatest friend you'll ever know.... Amen.

BACK THEN

Remember all those care-free days, when we were still at school,
How the teacher used to punish us if we should act the fool.
And remember Sunday mornings, we were made to dress up grand,
And off we'd march to Sunday School with Bible in our hand.
But I look around at how things changed, and it almost breaks my
heart,
Our community was our Universe and Our Churches played a part.
We cared about our neighbours, and knew them all by name,
But when we turn our back to God, It's never quite the same.
We cannot even speak His name, for fear we'll cause offence,
And yet they deem it progress, when to me it makes no sense.
The law that's meant to serve us, to worship as we please,
It seems would rather silence us, and bring us to our knees.
So, give me back the good old days, the good times and the bad,
And the Sunday school that I went to when I was just a lad.
To the times when we respected God, and knew His word as truth,
To the sound of all those hymns we sang,
that almost raised the roof....Amen.

TELL

If you find yourself in places unfamiliar, in
places you have never been before,
Confronted by strange faces you don't recognize,
second guessing what the future has in store.
If you're usually surrounded by companions, but
suddenly you're left all on your own,
If you've always dwelt within your limitations, but
this time you're outside your comfort zone.

Would you conform to others expectations, or
simply be the one that never wins?
Blend into surroundings like a chameleon, or know
where falsehood ends, and truth begins
If you disagreed with comments made by others, do
you think you'd have the courage so to say,
Even though you run the risk of being ostracised,
is that a price that your prepared to pay.

For I believe it's only right and proper, to always
wear our heart upon our sleeve,
To cling unto our every firm conviction and
be faithful to all that we believe.
So I place my trust in Jesus Christ, my Saviour,
to give me strength so I won't shy away,
In standing tall no matter where I'm standing
and tell of all He does for me each day.

For I feel this World today in which we're dwelling,
is so in need of many faithful hearts,
And we can't afford to suppress our inner feelings, when
each day it seems more love for Him departs,
So I'm prepared to stand my ground for Jesus,
and not just simply walk away or run,
And I'll proudly shout His message loud and clearly,
before we reach the point of no return.... Amen.

THE PROMISE

I could promise you I'll never sin again,
But I know the pledge would only be in vain.
For temptation follows me and I submit too easily,
When I know your blood will wash away the stain.

So I offer my repentance in a prayer,
For I believe it's only proper your aware,
Full of sorrow and remorse, for you help me stay the course
And I only seem to make it cause you're there.

So I ask you, please forgive me, I am weak,
I implore you give me all the strength I seek.
Oh if only it could be, that I could make you proud of me,
Then this life would be much brighter and less bleak......Amen

Bobbie Greer

HOME

A million stars adorn the evening sky, all created by our God on high,
Then along with all of this, He gave a world so full of bliss,
And someday I'll get to meet Him by and by.

He gave His Son by way of virgins' womb, who
died but left behind an empty tomb,
The one who loved the World so much, the
one with healing in His touch,
As we became His bride and He the groom

So no matter in this world where I may roam, I know
some day He'll come and lead me home,
Passing through the narrow gate, to a place well worth the wait.
Where every heart is polished bright as chrome.

Let us pray for sinners' souls that still are lost, as
we gather 'neath the shadow of the cross,
Let's be patient as we wait, soon we'll meet at Heaven's gate.
Where the joy we'll find, will be well worth the cost.......Amen.

THE JORDAN

The river looked so tranquil and appealing, not
a ripple on the water could be seen,
And not one single artist I'm aware of, could
capture such a sweet idyllic scene.
And we offered up our praise in celebration, as
we gathered there upon that river bank,
With our hands and eyes directed to the Heavens,
to glorify the God we had to thank.

For the place that we were gathered was the Jordan,
and I'd love to freeze that moment if I could,
For a perfect peace descended on my body, when I
shared the spot where John the Baptist stood.
We were assembled to fulfil a life's ambition, to
be Baptised in the same place as the Son,
So in turn we slowly entered Jordan's waters, as
the preacher called us forward one by one.

He offered up his arm as we approached him, with
the water that had crept up to our chest,
And though some may only see it as symbolic, we
gave thanks for just how richly we were Blessed.
Some may question all of our excitement, or
believe it doesn't merit all the fuss,
But we'll adhere to all the Jesus taught us and
carry out what He requires of us.

So I thank my God above for all He's given,
especially for His Son who bore my pain,
I'm so grateful that I've followed in His footsteps
and been baptised, so I've been born again.
So I'll look back on my memory of the Jordan, for its
trips like this that make our lives worthwhile,
And if my Saviour saw me in the waters, I trust that
He was watching with a smile.... Amen

THE SERMON

The sermon he delivered was astounding, with
words that only Heaven could anoint,
And the fire that raged within him so amazing, that
it felt like he was reaching boiling point.
The passion in his voice was so convincing, it was
as if the Lord had told him what to say,
As the Holy Spirit moved among those gathered,
and fifteen precious souls were won that day.

My heart was beating faster as I listened, I
couldn't move no matter how I'd try,
One minute I felt my cup was overflowing, the
next the tears were streaming from my eye.
My emotions were all taken on a journey,
an exhilarating roller coaster ride.
He controlled the very way that I was thinking,
and my feelings were impossible to hide.

And a hush descended on the congregation, as
in prayer he made his final Altar call,
And people raised their hands in total silence,
from every single section of the Hall,
Then I reached inside my pocket for a tissue, to
dry away the tears I could not stem,
And of those fifteen souls that then came forward, I'm
so proud to say that I was one of them.... Amen.

GUILTY

Is it really any wonder I feel guilty, when I
realise how much you gave for me?
As I, a sinner and so many like me, watched your
crimson blood flow down that tree.
Is it really any wonder I feel guilty, that's
the question I must pose again?
When every time I see the Cross of Calvary, it
reminds me of your suffering and pain.

The agony that must have wrecked your body, the
open wounds where nails were driven in,
The crown of thorns the soldiers placed upon you,
you suffered this to take away my sin.
The horror that I witnessed was appalling, and
to this day I feel my stomach churn,
When all I have to offer is my worship, oh
what a paltry offering in return.

But yet you could have stopped it in an instant, and
summoned hordes of Angels from the skies,
Yet instead because the sins of Men were many,
such cruelty took place before our eyes.
But it helps when I remember your in Heaven, the
scars are healed, there's no more blood or pain.
And in truth I take my greatest consolation, in the
knowledge you are coming back again.... Amen.

THE WINE

In producing wine the grapes may well be bitter, but
regardless we still pluck them from the vine,
We use them to their very best advantage, as
some of them produce the finest wine.
And that can be the way it is with Jesus, we should
maximise the gifts that we've been sent,
For given time our goodness starts to surface,
and the bitterness will go as we ferment.

So maybe at this moment you feel useless, and
nothing ever works out like it should,
But God will never leave you nor forsake you, and
all things come together for His good.
For each and every one of us have talent, we've
all a contribution we can make,
So if you think that you're the one exception,
that my friend would be a great mistake.

Just maybe you're a newly planted seedling, and
He feels it right to give you time to grow,
But when He feels the time is right to harvest, that
my friend is when He'll let you know.
So just be patient, wait until He calls you, and
lets you know the plans He has for you,
For its waste to pluck the grapes before their ready, let
His will determine when your time is due.... Amen.

213

BACKSLIDEN

He'd gave his heart to Jesus as a youngster,
since he was just a boy of only ten.
But as the years went by his love diminished, so much
water flowed beneath the bridge since then.
He felt his love for Jesus made no difference, since
the time that both his parents passed away,
Then he lost his job and struggled with his family
in settling all the bills they had to pay.

And every day there seemed to be new problems,
he felt like he was living with a curse,
Trying to raise his two sons and a daughter, with
every day the problems getting worse.
So where was God when He was really needed,
He hasn't really helped me since I've grown,
I am standing here with all my hope abandoned,
so it seems that I must do it all alone.

But then by chance he met up with his pastor, the
one who that day led him to the Lord,
And as both of them were really in no hurry, the
two of them then stopped to have a word
When the pastor heard about all his dilemmas, he
searched until the proper words he found,
It wasn't God who abandoned you my Brother,
in truth it was the other way around

The only one that God has turned His back on,
was His only Son that day at Calvary.
When He turned His head away with deepest sorrow,
as our Saviour gave His life for you and me.
And I remember as a boy there in my office, when
Jesus spoke and how you heard His call.
So bear in mind when problems start to surface, that's
the time we need Him most of all.... Amen.

THE COURTROOM

No-one can be certain of tomorrow, so it's
possible we've seen our last sun set,
For none of us are privy to the future, so this
may be the last chance that you get,
Have you taken time to put your house in order, and
planned ahead to show that you have cared?
If you haven't now's the time to ask the question, if
the Saviour calls your name are you prepared.

For the candle that's our life won't burn forever, it
grows shorter with each day that passes by,
For as sure as Man is given birth of Woman, just
as sure there comes his time to die,
So when the light we shine on Earth has been extinguished,
and we face our final judgement as we must,
Then the soul we have must make a final journey,
when our body's ash to ash and dust to dust.

So I wonder when you stand before the Father, just
the two of you in Heavens judgement hall,
When He looks back at the life that you were given,
will He recognise you loved Him after all.
But if you haven't gave your heart to Jesus,
or never really paid it any thought.
Remember that He gave His life at Calvary, so your
passageway to Heaven could be bought.... Amen

WORRY

Worry's never solved a single problem, stress
can see you in an early grave,
But prayer is a weapon much more powerful
and Jesus is the only one can save.
So when you find your burdens are too heavy,
pack them up and lay them at His feet,
His loving arms are there to lift and hold you, by
His mercy He can turn a sour life sweet.

And if you feel you're stuck in isolation, like a
stranger passing through a foreign land,
Just reach out and He will be there waiting,
ever there to take you by the hand.
For my scourge of loneliness has now departed,
that day he came and took away my sin,
When I felt like I was living in a bubble,
forever on the outside looking in.

We could search the World and never find an
answer, in many situations we've been placed,
But the rock of my Salvation is my courage.
in every problem I have ever faced.
I can welcome in each morning that He grants me,
in assurance that He watches over me,
I'm protected in the palm of my Lord Jesus, by
the hand that can calm the roughest sea.

The Saviour that I have is ever present and I've
relied on Him one hundred thousand times,
And although I was a Hell deserving sinner, I'm
aware that I'm forgiven of my crimes.
Yes, sometimes we believe that life is easy, but
only when the wind is at our back,
But all too quickly it can change direction, and we
find its God's protection that we lack.... Amen.

THE CHAIN

When we give our hearts to Jesus, we are links that form a chain,
Empowered by the blood of Christ, who did not die in vain.
Recipients of mercy, while we plead in His name's sake,
A chain so strongly bonded, that not a thing can break.

So let us come together, so His church is unified,
And send our love to the one we serve, so cruelly crucified.
Yet never be downhearted, be the link that never gives,
Don't let the cross distract you, just be grateful He still lives.

We are welded by His love for us, we can handle any strain,
And Satan, once defeated, will be defeated once again.
We will carry Jesus Standard, as we take to battlefield,
Where Faith will be the sword we bear, and Grace will be our shield.

The chains cannot be broken, once the links are all in place,
Forged by justice, fired by Faith, and tempered by His grace.
So, lets link arms together, Let His standard be unfurled,
And form a chain unbreakable, that encircles all the World....Amen.

JUDAS

For a purse containing thirty silver pieces,
treachery unequalled would be bought,
For that's the price that Judas placed on Jesus, in
spite of everything that he was taught.
He sat around the table with the others, with
only pure deception in his head,
But displayed no worthy reason for suspicion, as
he listened to each word his Master said.

He drank from the cup that Jesus placed before
him, as phony tears began to fill his eyes,
He ate the bread along with all the others, but
the feelings he displayed were only lies.
But deep inside he must have known his secret,
could not be hidden from the Son of Man,
For he was just a player, but essential, who
had a part to play in a Fathers plan.

So with the others deep in conversation, he
scurried off like a thief into the night,
But darkness could not hide him from a Saviour,
when nothing can be hidden from His sight.
And of every act of treason that ever happened,
I can truly think of none as cruel as this,
When he led the Roman soldiers to Gethsemane, and
there betrayed his Master with a kiss...Amen

UNIFIED

Put away the rosary and the candles, for all
those man-made trappings are absurd,
Just focus our attention on the Bible, for that's
where God has given us His word.
If you care to look, you'll see that pride divides us, for
we allow our stubbornness to hide the truth,
Then we criticise all other congregations, because
they worship underneath a different roof.

But this is not the way the Lord intended, to see a
splintered Church must make Him weep,
It's time to put a stop to all the bickering, and
end all those divisions running deep,
For you'll find there's no distinctions made in Heaven,
where the Lord knows everyone of us by name,
And whether you're a Cardinal or layman,
everyone is treated just the same.

The Lessons Jesus taught us were so simple, as His
Father gave commandments cast in stone,
So all we have to do to earn His favour, Is to
be a church that He will not disown.
And then we'll really start to feel His Glory, as
we recognise His many wondrous gifts,
And all we have to do is come together, and maybe
we can finally heal the rifts.... Amen.

DELIVERED

As I travel through this life that I've been given, the
knowledge that I hold just makes me smile,
For I know that I am travelling as a pilgrim, but my
real home's drawing closer mile by mile.
I have sampled all the pleasures life can offer, and
I've had my share of anguish on the way,
But my home is not on Earth it lies in Heaven, and
I know that I will get there one fine day.

For the soul that I was given, I returned it, when
Jesus plucked me out from all the crowds,
And when I reach my final destination, I will meet
with Him somewhere beyond the clouds.
Then my days of pain and anguish will be over,
those trials that took their toll upon my face.
Where the joy I find is beyond all comprehension,
as choirs of Angels sing Amazing Grace.

You may see this worn out body that I dwell in,
but it serves me only for my time on Earth,
For I know it's just my soul that is Eternal, from
that day when I was given second birth.
So whatever time the Lord above may grant me,
I'll be satisfied and ask Him for no more,
For my time on Earth will pale to insignificance,
compared to all the wonders that's in store...Amen.

ACCEPT

Jesus is the only route to Heaven, the only
gate that allows us to pass through,
For His words recorded in the Holy Bible, so
none can ever claim they never knew.
If you ask Him in your life, you'll be uplifted, He
will melt away your worry and your strife,
There's such honesty in every word He's spoken, When
He said He was the way, the truth, the life.

And, if after all He said your still a sceptic, then I
ask you let His words become the prod,
To remove all doubt if you still need convincing,
That He was indeed the only Son of God.
For none can even dream to match His wisdom,
and to tell His story where would I begin?
We are all so much in need of His forgiveness, with
every one of us completely drenched in sin.

So, we only have to grasp the hand on offer, the
hand He's holding out to you and me,
For we're incarcerated by the sin we carry, let His
word become the truth that sets us free.
You will feel at last that you've been liberated, and
the changes in your life will leave you shocked,
But the day that you accept Him as your Saviour, you will
find the gate to Heaven's been unlocked.... Amen.

THE DECISION

I sometimes speculate about the future,
especially at the closing of each day,
And I think about the moment I'll meet Jesus,
and wonder what exactly I will say.
Will the shame of how I've lived just leave me
speechless, Will I look into His eyes or turn away?
Will I fall down on my knees and ask forgiveness
and plead at Heaven's gate so I can stay.

Have I done enough to satisfy His Father, will
He grant me all the mercy that I seek,
Or will the catalogue of sin of which I'm guilty,
be the barrier that will not let me speak.
Could any words I use convey my sorrow, or
convince Him of how foolish I have been,
When He watched me in my days before I met Him,
and my every misdemeanour He has seen.

I can only throw myself upon His mercy, and
trust He'll show compassion undeserved,
And should He hold out both His arms in welcome,
then I'll know my place in Heaven is reserved.
I must apologise if you find my story frightening,
but I felt that it was something I must tell,
For I'd rather frighten someone into Heaven, than
watch them marching blindly into hell...Amen

WHEN HEAVEN CALLS

Although we all enjoy a little sunshine, just
relaxing as we bask beneath its glow,
But remember we're dependent on the harvest, and
it take the showers of rain to make it grow.
And likewise, we'll experience discomfort, that
we would make to vanish if we could,
But the more the bad times come and pay a visit,
the more that we appreciate the good.

There'll be days when mountains seem to rise before us,
when we think our tears are never going to dry,
And there'll be days when we direct our gaze to
Heaven, to thank the Lord for helping us get by.
But the days we spend on Earth will have their
limit, for no-one gets to live for evermore,
And when Heaven calls, we'll stand in pure amazement,
at the wonders and the Glory waiting there.

For not an eye on Earth can visualise it, there'll be
sounds that Earthly ears cannot perceive,
As Our Father takes away our former torment,
and the only thing He asks is we believe.
So, the next time that the storm clouds start to
gather, so much so that they blot out the Sun,
Remember what your facing's not Eternal, just think
about those wondrous days to come...Amen

CHILDREN

Of all the blessings God above has granted, like the way He lifts me
every time I fall,
I believe with all my heart from what He's given, our children are the
richest gift of all.
For I know they are a present straight from Heaven, like a Rainbow
forming after we've had rain,
And a sign He's still abiding by our covenant, that
His hand will not destroy the world again.
But it's up to us as parents how we raise them, that's it's from Him
alone we see all goodness stem,
That they should never take the love of God for granted, but
appreciate His blessings gave to them.
We should encourage them to read the Holy Bible, and it's essential
that we teach them how to pray,
To acknowledge sin and always ask forgiveness, and
that His love for us keeps growing every day.
We should explain to them how they have got two Fathers, one on
Earth, and one who dwells above,
And the one in Heaven cares for them so deeply, that He sacrificed
His Son to show His love,
So, maybe if we set a good example, when we discover that our
children all have grown,
They'll remember all the lessons that we taught them, and
God willing, teach the children of their own....Amen.

THE RETURN

We are so in need of Jesus, the more that I explore,
This generation needs Him, like it's never done before.
We have hunger and starvation, while evil's running rife,
And Man, it seems, has lost respect for the sanctity of life.

The rich are getting richer, while the poor are on their knees,
And the stench of death that stems from war is carried on the breeze.
Our young have fallen victim as addictions start to grow,
Respect for parents disappeared a long, long time ago.

But we know the Lords returning, and that day is drawing near,
And all the signs would indicate that time is almost here.
For evil must be challenged, and not be left unchecked,
So, goodness may return again, like honour, love, respect.

Soon our chains will all be broken, no longer we'll be bound,
I will lift my gaze to Heaven when I hear the trumpet sound.
It will signal His arrival, He will walk on Earth again,
All evil will be vanquished, when our Saviour comes to reign.... Amen

SERVANT

Here I stand before you as a servant, Just a
sinner so unworthy of your pain,
Yet I recognise that I'm so undeserving, for you
know that I could never be that vain.
And the stripes that they inflicted on your body,
every one of them you took because of me,
It was my sin that kept you hanging there at Calvary,
where you gave your life to set this sinner free.

I now understand the reason why you perished, and
I'm grateful that you went there all the same,
But the debt I owe is more than I can offer, and
thus I have to hang my head in shame.
For the sacrifice required could have no blemish,
and only you my Lord could fit the bill,
And though you cried out for your Fathers mercy,
it was left to you to carry out His will.

And when we heard you mutter "it is finished",
when death had put a halt to all your pain,
We could not know that only three days later, you
would leave the tomb and walk on Earth again.
Now the cost of sin is stricken from the record,
the blood you shed enough to pay the bill,
And forever as your servant I am grateful, for that
price you paid upon Golgotha's Hill......Amen

THE FRIEND

As I drove to church one wet and windy morning,
I saw a figure huddled at the door,
And as I approached him with a sense of caution,
I enquired of him what he was looking for.
He answered He was waiting for the service, I
was worried, but he told me he was fine,
His head was bowed but suddenly he raised it,
until his eyes were looking into mine.

He told me that he loved to hear the service, but
at the doors where he preferred to stay.
For the clothes he wore were really not that suitable,
and his shoes were only fit to throw away.
But in his eyes the truth was more revealing, it was
embarrassment, that kept him waiting there,
And the idea of him of sitting next to others was a
thought that he was not prepared to bear.

And in an instant, I recalled the words of Jesus,
"I was a stranger and yet you welcomed me"
And I took my new found brother by the shoulder
and asked him if he'd like to sit by me.
So together we enjoyed that Sunday morning,
as we listened so intently side by side,
Now I meet with him each week and we give worship,
so grateful he no longer has to hide...Amen.

DECISIONS

I wonder what decisions will be required of me today,
Choices seem to rule our lives, that's always been the way.
From the moment we awaken, and we open up our eyes,
Do we have the time to snooze a while, or is it time to rise?

We decide the things we want to eat, the clothes we want to wear
Our comings and our goings, and the way we wear our hair.
Our decisions impact others, as we travel through each day,
For we decide when the time is right for us to go or stay.

But the one decision that I took, that I do not regret,
That stands above all others and I never will forget.
Was the day I took a Saviour, as I knelt upon my knees,
And He came and took my sin away, as easy as you please.

I just regret the many years, I now consider waste,
How I made such rash decisions, with so many made in haste
But there's sound advice now given, from
The Lord who won't forsake,
For He's there to help and guide me, with
each decision that I make.... Amen

MIRACLES

If I could see a miracle, perhaps then I'd believe,
The words of those without The Lord, so blinded and naive.
If only they possessed some faith, and for that I must pray,
For miracles surround us and are happening every day.

The stars that fill the evening sky, are a sign of Heavens Grace,
It's the hand of God that created them and holds them all in place.
The beauty of the forests, who's branches touch the sky,
The wonders of the oceans, all the works of God on high.

The Sun that spreads its golden rays, to give us light on Earth,
The healing touch for those in pain, the miracle of birth.
The fields that give up all their yield, providing us with food,
The silver lining of that cloud, transforming bad to good.

The laughter of our children, the gift of each new day,
The knowledge someone's listening, when we take the time to pray.
You already have your miracles, they're right in front of you.
It's just your lack of faith my friend, that hides
them from your view.... Amen.

STRENGTH

If surrounded by my enemies, they will not see me flinch,
With a Faith so firmly grounded, that I won't concede an inch,
For my strength I draw from Jesus, from the power of His name,
Whose forgiveness was essential, breaking through my Veil of Shame.
I have made Him many promises, but every time fall short,
Yet He's promised to forgive me, when I'm standing in His court.
Through my weakness, I'm a failure, I forever let Him down,
Still He offers His forgiveness, with the promise of a crown.
I have given my allegiance, when I called Him and He came,
And I will serve no other, for there is no other name.
I'm a witness to His Glory with intentions that are pure,
But if only I was stronger, to avoid temptations lure.
I can only say I'm sorry, and exhibit true remorse,
But I need Him there beside me, to assist me in life's course.
And I'll always do the best I can, for the one who set me free,
Let Him touch this heart and remove the sin,
that still abides in me....Amen.

CHANGED

When a heart is cleansed of all its sin, it creates a little space,
Where faith and trust come rushing in, to occupy its place.
And the difference is apparent, for all who care to look,
That you've become a different person, with that first step you took.

Some may hold you up to ridicule, by slandering your name,
Or attempt to convince the friends you
have, your nothing like you claim.
You'll experience rejection, but the truth will always tell,
Just cast your mind to Jesus, He dealt with this as well.

But the strength that you've been given, is enough to see you through,
For you'll never have a cross to bear, you deem too much for you.
And the stress that you encounter, given time, will melt away.
As you gain respect from everyone, you meet along your way.

They will see the Child of God in you, and know your love is deep,
For we can tell a lot about others by the company they keep.
They will see how much you love Him, by the passion in your voice,
And how a sinner's life was changed, that day
you made your choice.... Amen.

CHILDREN

We should listen more to children, and take time to reflect,
For words of wisdom often stem, from a source we least expect.
Perhaps it's out of innocence, they tend to simplify,
But they never over analyse as much as you and I.

When we tell them Jesus loves them, they accept it to be true,
They will never question motives, the way we seem to do.
They place their trust more easily, believing what we say,
Enthusiastic, keen to learn. forgiving come what may.

They accept the Bible stories, that we teach them at our knee,
Don't look for flaws, that may give cause, to make them disagree.
They display a sense of reverence, as their kneeling down to pray.
When they know the Lord is listening to every word they say.

They adopt to change more easily, that comes as no surprise,
If only it was possible, to see things through their eyes.
So, when God calls us His Children, after we've been born anew,
Perhaps we should behave like them and not the way we do...Amen.

WHO

Who decides the moment of when we're born or when we die,
Who provides the strength we need to help us all get by,
And who's the one we turn to, when toils become too much,
Who's the one protecting us, with healing in His touch.

Who provides direction, should we ever go astray,
And who is so forgiving, He still loves us anyway
Who remains beside us, when our so-called friends depart,
Who picks up the pieces of a badly broken heart?

Who provides our sustenance, with gift of daily bread?
Who shows us there's a better way with every word He said,
Whose love is so unmeasurable, that he gave for us His Son,
The answer's unequivocal, I believe there's only one.

Our Father up in Heaven, for He does all this and more,
He brought a sense of purpose to where
only heartaches dwelt before.
He opened up a prison cell, and set the prisoner free,
Of this I am so certain, for that prisoner was me.... Amen

SERVANT

What a privilege to serve the Lord, in any way I can,
With my life at His disposal, I await His next command.
I will follow where He leads me, neither pause nor hesitate,
Finding comfort in the knowledge, only He controls my fate.

I will humbly kneel before Him, as I'm placed before His throne,
For I'm a child that He created, with His Son my cornerstone.
I am built on firm foundation, in His arms I'm ever safe,
For the bricks were my conviction, and the mortar is my faith.

May the love that I have found in Him, keep growing, never lapse,
For His Kingdom is eternal, while the others all collapse.
For as long as I am capable, I will labour in His field,
With His truth my suit of armour, and His mercy as my shield.

What a privilege to serve my God, who's love for me is great,
And I pray that when He calls me home, it's through the narrow gate.
And when I enter Heaven, there I'll see my great reward,
From the one that I was proud to serve,
the one I call My Lord....Amen.

FOUND

For all that I believe in, I'm prepared to stand my ground,
Defending to my final breath, the Glory I have found.
I will not fail nor falter, as I travel life's terrain,
Through all the days I'm granted, in His service I'll remain.

I will wear His badge with honour, for all He's done for me,
In the hope of changing many minds, of those who'd disagree.
May my words become a beacon, shining, bringing forth such light,
To lead them from their darkness, to the presence of His sight.

There are individual people, with individual needs,
But all of these are laid to rest, once Jesus intercedes.
He has led me to green pastures, beside a babbling brook,
I've became a different person, if you'll take the time to look,

And because of all the joy I have, it's only fair I tell,
That it's waiting there for you to claim. so you can share as well,
Your past can be forgiven, by the precious blood He shed,
You'll feel His Grace, He'll help you face,
the days that lie ahead.... Amen.

WOLVES

We've been warned of those approaching, as
wolves dressed in sheep's clothes,
Who will have their own agenda and no conscious I suppose?
They'll appear so sugar coated, on the surface it might seem,
But underneath their wicked and will shatter every dream.

There will be many falling victim, to the lies their being fed,
Condemned to forfeit Heaven and so easily mislead.
Confused by so called prophets, who've abandoned all the truth,
Who'll contaminate the scriptures, where there isn't any proof.

These days we must be vigilant, and careful where we tread,
Trusting not in others, but in Jesus Christ instead.
For there's a hill outside Jerusalem, where a rugged cross once stood,
Where the blood of Jesus saved us, the only one who could.

Just adhere to Jesus message, ignore false teachings getting rife,
For He told us very clearly, He's the way, the truth, the life.
And none shall enter Heaven, on that most Glorious of days,
By listening to false prophets or following their ways......Amen.

AN HOUR

If I asked, would you come along with me,
we will just be gone an hour,
And you might enjoy the worship, and the singing of the choir.
What else would you be doing, but watching some T.V,
When it would be more beneficial, if you came along with me.

We can listen to the sermon, based on all that Jesus told,
But be sure you bring a hat and coat, outside it's getting cold.
And maybe, only maybe, when they reach the altar call,
You'll be enlightened by the message and make sense of it all.

For it's all about a Saviour, who gave His life for me,
Who paid the price for all my sin, at a place called Calvary?
And His story is a precious one, that everyone should hear
If it wasn't for His sacrifice, You and I would not be here.

So, the least that we can do for Him, is a small price in return,
For He saved us from the fires of Hell, ensuring we don't burn.
So, grab you coat and follow, and leave the warmth of that cosy fire.
And because of all He's done for us, will you
invest with just one hour? Amen.

THE VISIT

If you hear a gentle whisper, break the silence of the night,
That tells you not to worry, everything will be alright.
Then you feel a hand upon you, that makes you wonder how,
With a touch so warm and tender as it gently wipes your brow.

You may even see a shadow, though it causes you no fear,
Or hear the swishing of a gown and feel there's someone near.
Is it just imagination when you feel that you've been kissed,
With emotions overloaded that make you powerless to resist.

Did you smell the scent of flowers, did their aroma fill the air?
Maybe movement in a corner, that made you stop and stare.
Did you feel a sense of calmness, hear the
blood rush through your veins?
And though it lasted but a second, still the thought of it remains.

If this is all familiar, then I'm not on my own,
It's how conviction calls to us, when we are all alone.
It's the sound of Jesus calling, to try and change our fate
For I believe with all my heart, it's how He'll communicate.... Amen

ARRIVAL

I cannot help but wonder, will the clocks no longer chime,
When my time is up, and I close my eyes for the very final time,
Will there be a new beginning, when my days on Earth are through?
Will my days be so much different, to the ones that I once knew?

Will I be aboard a vessel, in a very different realm,
With my fellow passengers dressed in white, and Jesus at the helm.
Will a fair wind blow to guide us, 'til our sails can hold no more?
Will we cry in celebration, when we dock on Heavens shore?

Or will I rise up like an eagle, through clouds so white they blind,
Will I stare down in amazement, at the world I've left behind.
Will I soar among the Angels, hear the beating of their wings?
And be completely breathless, sampling all that Heaven brings.

Or maybe there'll be music, as sweet as it can be,
With one hundred thousand voices, all there to welcome me.
And if the gate is open, then their sound will guide me in,
And all because of Jesus, who has washed away my sin.... Amen

TIMES

There are times we need to follow, and times that we must lead,
There are times that we must air our views
that's how we plant His seed.
There are times we must be silent, and times we need to speak,
And times we need to journey, when in search of all we seek.

There are times to share with others, how the love of God is found,
And times we need to call on Him and lay our burdens down.
There are times we must be thankful, that He took away our shame,
And times to stop and wonder at the Glory of His name.

There are times to teach our children, how
to worship Him with praise,
Ensuring as their parents, they are brought up in His ways.
There are times to read His Holy word, and do all that it asks,
And time to shed a tear or two, through the hardship of our tasks.

But above all, please remember, that the time is drawing near,
When the clouds will start to open up and Jesus will appear.
So use your time up wisely, or to your cost you'll find,
That the trumpet sounds its warning, and
you've ran out of time.... Amen.

SHARE

Revelation speaks, of how things look, when we reach the final days,
And everything we see and hear, conforms to what it says.
There's vanity, profanity, debauchery and sin,
No caring and no sharing, so the ice is wearing thin.

But let's not be disheartened, for hope is yet at hand,
For Jesus is returning soon, to reign in every land.
My faith is truly anchored in the one who never fails,
And after all is said and done, I know His will prevails.

Yet we all have a duty, as the pardoned and the saved,
To spread His message far and wide, to those as yet enslaved.
For the fires in Hell are burning, for souls containing stains,
And Jesus is the only key to free them from their chains.

So, time may well be limited, for the countdown has begun,
So never rest or tarry, until we've freed them everyone.
For we must remove the blinkers, so that every eye might see,
One word might make the difference, to
where they spend eternity.... Amen.

Bobbie Greer

ACCEPT

If your hiding from your worries in the hope that they will pass,
Maybe staring at the bottom of another empty glass.
Is the race of life so torturous, you'll never reach the tape?
So, you've turned to drugs and alcohol, as a method of escape.

If you go to bed each evening, with a sigh of sheer relief,
That you've made it through another day, by soaking up your grief.
If you've reached the point you're questioning,
the very point of living,
Or feel you've drawn the short straw, with
the life that you've been given.

Well, life is what we make it, each decision bears a price,
And we really only start to live, once we've accepted Christ.
Life can throw up problems, that leave us feeling numb,
And though we cannot change the past, we can the days to come.

For I once stood where you are, so I know just how you feel,
But I gave my life to Jesus and the scars began to heal.
So, you can come and join us, for I know He'll welcome you,
And the grey skies of the life you lead,
tomorrow will be blue.... Amen.

FORGIVE

Should others point the finger, out of total disrespect,
Or aim their poisoned arrows, not that easy to deflect,
Though it's hard when you're the target, of
someone you thought you knew,
When their holding onto weapons and aiming them at you.

But life is never easy, when you give your life to Christ,
You must rise above the challenge, be prepared to pay that price.
For when Jesus dwells within you, your never quite alone,
So, let the one who's without sin, be first to cast the stone.

He taught us when we take a blow, to turn the other cheek,
For suffering can multiply, while it's revenge, we seek.
Instead we should forgive those, who'd wish to do us harm,
Treat them like a Brother and extend to them your arm.

And soon you'll see a change of heart, as all the conflict ends.
And those you thought your enemies, will soon become your friends,
Let love become the thread we need for friendships that were torn.
For when we respect each other's views,
true fellowship is born.... Amen.

MY ALL

In sickness my physician, who enables me to heal,
In despair you are my comforter, who knows just how I feel.
My protector when in danger, you're the cleft in which I hide,
You're my guard against temptation, when
I'm lost, you'll be my guide.

My provider, you sustain me, with the gift of daily bread,
My resting place when needed, where I rest my weary head.
The rock of my Salvation, every night and every day,
The forgiver of my many sins, that you have swept away.

My teacher, I'm forgiven by the lessons you have taught,
With a love so true and tender, that with money can't be bought.
When I need someone to hold me, you are there to fill the role,
You're the mender of a broken life, that somehow made me whole.

You're the giver, I'm the taker, all you ask is I believe,
You empowered me with wisdom, when I was so naive.
You are walking right beside me, where-soever I should roam.
And when my days are over, by your Grace
you'll lead me home.... Amen.

JOHN

His nickname was "The Preacher", though in truth his name was John,
His platform was that wooden box he always stood upon.
At a stadium or marketplace, John was always there,
Reciting from the Bible as he waved it in the air.

Wherever crowds were gathered, it was there that he would stand.
Reaching out to others with that bible in his hand.
His words were so emotional, though his voice was growing faint,
And though few would stop to listen, He'd the patience of a Saint.

And each and every Saturday, he set his box in place,
As the market filled with shoppers, He wore a smile upon his face,
For surely with so many, there may just be souls to win.
And one or two may heed his words and repent of all their sin.

But that was his last sermon, for the Lord then called him home,
To take his place in Heaven, no more markets would he roam,
But I think of those who listened, who I believe by now are gone,
And do they now abide in Heaven, all thanks
to "Preacher" John....Amen.

THE OFFER

He delivered many promises, and every one He's kept,
Now He's holding out His hand to you, are you ready to accept?
Will you take the hand on offer, is this your defining day?
For just one touch from Jesus and your Sins are swept away.

He can bring a new-found purpose to a life that's in a mess,
So, when He whispers, "do you love me",
just make sure the answers yes.
No-one is excluded from the love He has to share,
You only need to close your eyes and He'll be waiting there.

Was there ever any other, who could offer you so much,
Who took those nails at Calvary, yet forgives us by His touch?
Who shed His blood so willingly, to prove how much He cared,
So, we could gain eternal life in the mansion He's prepared.

So, think before you answer, when He offers up His hand,
Ponder on His sacrifice, make sure you understand.
Our lives unfurl before us, by the decisions that we take,
But this is the most important one, that you will ever make.... Amen.

AGEING

It was never my intention, ambition nor desire,
For I thought my life was perfect, and I couldn't climb much higher.
But that was in my younger days, such foolish things I said,
'til I realized I needed help for the days that lay ahead

For my years were quickly mounting, and time does not stand still,
Worldly pleasures disappeared and somehow lost their thrill.
But I was looking to the future, not the memories of the past,
I was in need of reassurance as my years were passing fast.

For I looked around at faces, older now if truth be told,
And I realized I was one of them and also getting old.
So, I clasped my hands together, dropped to my knees to pray,
I was like a candle burning, growing shorter day by day.

And as I finished off my prayer, I felt a sense of peace,
As though I'd been a prisoner and been granted my release.
So, my steps might start to falter, but I will not shed a tear,
For I know now Heaven waits for me and
is ever drawing near.... Amen.

THE STORM

When you hear the storm approaching, are
you sure your house will stand,
Is it built on firm foundations, on the rock and not the sand?
For the winds that blow will test it, as the rains come pouring down,
So be sure it's planted firmly on The Saviours Holy ground.

Ensure that your materials were founded in the truth,
May the love of God be present, from foundations to the roof.
May He ever be your shelter, so His arms will keep you warm.
As He offer's His protection, in the face of any storm.

Be resolute in all you do, and let storm subside,
Be confident that Jesus is forever by your side.
For storms won't last forever and very soon they'll pass,
The Sun will start to shine again, with dew upon the grass.

Yes, the storms of life may test us, But by the Grace of God,
We're protected as His children, on every road we trod.
For the blood of Christ protects us, by the power it contains,
And the strongest tempest dies away, but
His truth still remains.... Amen

FUTURE

My greatest expectation, to make this world a better place,
Is that nations come together, so Revival gathers pace.
Then divisions can be ended, we can worship all as one,
And there can be a new beginning, once the healing has begun.

When all will bow to Jesus, what a marvellous sight to see,
As, to acknowledge all His glory, every nation bows the knee.
When colour will not matter, nor age nor sex nor creed,
Just voices raised in unison, as the kind of the start we need.

And we'll feel the Lords approval, when
He sees what we've achieved,
A world of firm conviction, where everyone believed.
Yes, all of this is possible, if we only have desire,
For God will give encouragement and fill our hearts with fire.

And we'll send our praise to Heaven, as all borders disappear,
There'll be an end to pointless suffering, and an end to war and fear.
Then our children can inherit, this world of which I tell,
And see what God has done for us, and
worship Him as well.... Amen.

THE CROSS

When a tragedy comes calling, and you think that life's unfair,
Or you see someone in perfect bliss and wish that you were there.
But we only see the surface and not what's deep inside,
And the difference separating us, is their ability to hide.

Far off fields look greener, but in truth are just the same,
And life can throw up incidents where no-one is to blame.
It's really how we handle these, in a church or in a bar,
And how we deal with good and bad, that makes us who we are.

So, if your searching in a bottle, you need to be aware,
That when you awake next morning, the problem is still there.
But if you look to Jesus, when all else was in vain,
He will help to ease your burdens, and He'll take away the pain.

If your trapped in some dark tunnel, or when troubles lie in store,
He will lead you out the other end much stronger than before.
We've all a cross to carry, regrettable but true,
But the heaviest cross is due to sin, and
He carried that for you.... Amen

FREED

Come into my parlour said the spider to the fly,
And so, it is with Satan, for every trick he'll try.
He's guaranteed to try all means to trap you in his snare,
But all too soon you'll realise, there's no way out of there.

There is one source of protection, to thwart his little game,
He's the guard against temptation, and Jesus is His name.
He will tear you from the clutches and free you from your cell,
He will raise you from all evil just as though you never fell.

He'll remove the poisoned chalice, Satan raised up to your lip,
He will take you to His bosom, and never let you slip.
He'll remove all your addictions, help you overcome all fears,
Give you back your life again for all those wasted years.

You only have to call on Him, if you're in Satan's hold,
He will break the chains that bind you, exactly as He's told.
For your sin is all forgiven, when the Son has set you free,
So, get behind me Satan, I've the Lord protecting me.... Amen.

AWARE

He knows the darkest secrets that lie buried in your mind,
He's all seeing, He's all knowing, if it's hidden, He will find.
Not a single word or action can be hidden from His view,
He's observing, He's a witness, as He watches over you.

From the moment you accept Him and ask Him in your heart,
He will take away the sin you have and grant a brand-new start.
Temptations all around us, it exists to bring us down,
But through the Grace He offers you can turn your life around.

His arms are there to lean upon when the going gets too rough,
He'll grant you all the strength you need, if you don't have enough.
For He made us in His image, and He knows us all by name,
So, if we stray away from Him, it's only us to blame.

But in the end, we sink or swim, He's left us with that choice,
Will we take our pleasures from the world, or listen to His voice?
For many take the broadest road to places dark and dim,
But I will take the narrow route, that leads me safe to Him....Amen.

HOPE

The crown of thorns has withered, and the nails have turned to rust,
Though your trial's engrained in history, with its verdict so unjust.
Calvary's memory fading, for the cross no longer stands,
The scars by now have mended on both your feet and hands.

But after what they witnessed, and the crowds had all dispersed
Could they carry on just like before, with their lives so well-rehearsed
They had welcomed you a Saviour, then watched you as you died,
The hopes of many shattered as they watched you crucified,

They relied on you to overcome the hardships that they faced,
Were the words you used a smokescreen,
was their trust in you misplaced.
Would their future keep them underfoot, by the heel of Roman law?
Were they really so delusional, to clutch at any straw,

But when hearts are truly broken, and you've no more cards to play,
When you think you've been defeated, God will find a way.
For joy replaced dejection, when you overcame deaths snare,
Was a victory ever sweeter, that was born out of despair.... Amen.

FREE

Give only unto Caesar, that which Caesar's due,
For the Lord demands no payment for all He's given you.
For we cannot price forgiveness, and mercy bears no charge,
Were we to know how much we owe; the bill would be too large.
He only asks we trust Him, that's all we have to pay,
Yet He sent His Son to die for us, to wash our sin away.
But I know He's coming back again, He lives and did not die,
And we'll see the New Jerusalem, descending from the sky.

Soon the sound of Angel legions, will shake the very ground
As we all receive our mansions, for that's where they'll be found.
There, the ones who heard His calling, will see their just reward,
Amidst the cries of celebration, forever we'll be heard.

And the Earth will live in peace again, on that most Glorious day,
The sound of war will vanish as the guns are put away.
The deaf will get to hear again, the blind will get to see,
Whenever He returns again and claims the victory.... Amen

THE BLOOD

As our memories start to wither with every passing day,
And buildings start to crumble and fall into decay.
But I know that every drop of blood that was shed in that first hour,
Has never lost its potency and still retains its power.

It's the key to true forgiveness as it washes over you,
Removes all stains from blackened hearts, like nothing else can do.
It's a fountain freely flowing, that delivers up redemption,
It's the foe against all evil and the guard against temptation.

It's the only route to Heaven, if that is what you crave,
Sees you lifted up to Glory helps you overcome the grave.
Yes, the blood of Jesus cleanses, so what more need I say,
It was saving all those years ago and is saving to this day.

So, perhaps that was the reason that my Saviour came to die,
For it's because of all He suffered, that we have a great supply.
But you'll only feel its power, once Jesus you have found,
For Calvarys' cross ensured there is enough to go around.... Amen.

CELEBRATION

Has your life became a showcase for the faith that you proclaim?
Does your love for Jesus flourish, for there is no other name?
Are you prepared to shine a light for Him, no matter where you go?
Do you tell your friends you love Him so that all of them will know?

Will you hold aloft His banner, and proclaim Him King of Kings?
Will you march with Him to battle, knowing all the risk that brings?
Would you lay your life before Him, ignoring all that lies before?
And be contented in the knowledge He grants life for evermore.

Are you prepared to be His beacon, when all around grows dim?
Do you celebrate with vigour when another comes to Him?
Do you shed a tear in knowing. just how hot Hell's fires can burn,
As you gaze towards the heavens while awaiting His return.

Do you offer up a word of thanks, for the gift of each new day?
Knowing, by His blood, He paid the price, to wash your sin away.
Have you been lifted out of bondage, has He broken all your chains?
Were you a Hell deserving sinner, yet His
love for you remains...? Amen.

DISCIPLES

It only takes a single spark, to ignite a raging fire,
And just one word of encouragement can fulfil a heart's desire.
So just one Sun is all we need, to bring us heat and light,
And a lonely Moon that brightens up the very darkest night.

So if you open up a Bible, you won't have far to delve,
To see what was accomplished, by just the Lord and twelve.
For the world was changed forever, with a love that can't be bought,
And hope would rest eternal by the message that He brought.

There was Peter there was Andrew, fishermen of the sea,
And then came brothers James and John the sons of Zebedee.
Simon was the zealot, a tax collector named Matthew,
Judas who'd betray Him and then Bartholomew.

James the son of Alphaeus and Judas son of James,
There was Philip there was Thomas, and these were all their names.
They came from different backgrounds,
but they shared a common aim,
For the world that they have left behind,
would never be the same.... Amen

FOLLOW

If you've ever watched a Shepherd as he gathers up his sheep,
And how they choose to follow, with a trust that runs so deep.
And how a look of consternation seems to cut him to the core,
Causing bitter disappointment, when one's unaccounted for.

Well that's the way it is with Christ, He wants us as His own,
And like that shepherd of His flock, my trust in Him has grown.
And should I ever wander, throughout sunshine, wind or rain
I know that He'll coming searching, up until I'm found again.

So, when the going gets a little tough, you won't hear me complain,
When the odds are stacked against me, I will try and try again.
While I know the Lord is with me, I'll refuse to be perturbed
He won't leave me nor forsake me, For He's given me His word.

He led me from the wilderness and took me for His own,
Now all the problems facing me I won't face them alone.
I may not know the future nor what tomorrow brings,
But only that I'll face it with the Almighty King of Kings....Amen.

CREATION

On that first day of creation, out of darkness there came light,
Equal in proportion, separating day from night.
The second day gave atmosphere and the firmament set in place.
Created by the hand of God through His amazing grace.

On the third day all the land appeared, trees and plants of every kind,
On Day four the stars and planets were intricately aligned.
The fifth day gave us all the birds and fish that swelled the deep,
Day six He breathed life into man, and His work was near complete.

For He looked down on creation, and He saw that it was good,
And a universe was constructed, by the only one who could.
So the Seventh day He rested, after all His work was through,
And this world He manufactured, He then
gave to me and you.... Amen.

THANK YOU

For every hill you helped me climb, for every stream I've crossed,
For directions you have given me whenever I was lost
For being there in times of need, for listening while I pray,
For courage when I needed it and showing me the way.

For nursing me in sickness, and restoring me to health,
For always placing trust in me, when I didn't trust myself.
For your hand upon my shoulder, and urging me along,
For leading me to safety from where I did not belong.

And for that day I found you Lord, and You accepted me,
A sinner so unworthy but you must have heard my plea.
I called you and you answered, for I heard you as you neared,
And my sin was all forgiven, it so quickly disappeared.

Now I know that you abide in me, I was in need of your support,
And I know you'll show me mercy, when I'm standing in your court.
For I know you'll look upon me, on that day you find me there
And you'll Know how much I love you, so
your judgement will be fair.... Amen.

COME

When the hill that lies ahead of you, appears too steep to climb,
When you need to see the workload through,
but your running out of time.
If you find the load your carrying, is just too much to bear,
Cast your cares on Jesus, He's waiting for your prayer.

When you feel that your unworthy or consumed by angry mood,
If you've neglected doing many things, when
you know you really should,
If you miss someone who's passed away, and are grieving at their loss,
Gather up your worries and lay them at the cross.

If problems seem to shadow you and follow you around,
If your searching for companionship, but no-one's to be found.
When the game is almost over and your staring at defeat,
Bring your concerns to Jesus and lay them at His feet.

He will be your inspiration; He will help you start again.
He will offer consolation; He'll be there to ease your pain.
He will grant you all the strength you need
or provide much needed rest,
You may think you're undeserving, but He
loves you none the less.... Amen.

PERSECUTION

I thank you for the ability that allows me to decide,
And thanks for where you've placed me
Lord, in this land where I abide.
That I'm free to worship openly, with neither fear nor threat,
For the liberties bestowed on me, that are easy to forget.

For I cast my mind to far off lands, in this same world that we share,
And count my blessings every day that I am here, not there.
I see the persecution, of those who worship you,
And like a child I'm helpless, for there's nothing I can do.

I see how others suffer, yet they've done nothing wrong,
And wonder should I face the same, if I could be that strong.
The threat of death hangs over them, yet they don't release their hold,
And I doubt I'd have that courage, if the truth is to be told.

For my sisters and my Brothers, I'm so sorry for your plight,
I look on in admiration as you carry on your fight.
But I know the Lord is watching, and His grace will bring you through,
And when I get to Heaven, there I'll meet again with you....Amen.

THE CALL

They received that call they dreaded, and tears filled all their eyes,
They must gather at his bedside, to say their last goodbyes.
The treatment was exhausted, there was no more could be done,
And with heavy hearts they made their
way, his daughter, wife and son.

They held his hand and wiped his brow, though he was unaware,
Sedated and oblivious, that they were gathered there.
And they formed a little circle, and each took turns to pray,
That the hand of God might intervene, if there was any way.

And they spent another restless night all huddled around the phone,
Holding hands and praying, they would not hear its tone.
And the night passed by so slowly, and each hour felt like a year,
But the Lord would not forsake them, they
could feel Him drawing near.

Then the phone rang in the morning, it was the son who took the call,
They requested they return again, and they waited in the hall.
And a doctor saw them presently, bewildered and confused,
For a miracle had taken place, to which he wasn't used.

The signs were all improving, but he said reluctantly,
That there is no explanation, as to how this came to be.
But the family looked to Heaven, with each of them aware,
That this doctor underestimates, the power of a prayer.... Amen.

FREE

Tomorrow may bring laughter, or maybe floods of tears,
Anger, joy or memories of all my golden years.
But no matter what it holds for me, no matter what I face.
I know the Lord will be with me to guide me by His Grace.

For He said He'll never leave me, and that has proven true,
I can feel Him there beside me in everything I do.
And even when I get things wrong, He's willing to forgive,
So, the day you give your heart to Him, is the day you start to live.

Yes, I'm proud to follow Jesus, He's become my guiding star,
For its only through His mercy that I have come this far.
Without His hand to guide me, I'm afraid that I'd be lost,
For life can be demanding and I couldn't pay the cost.

But I'm thankful that I answered, when He called out my name,
For my life was changed forever and would never be the same.
He took the broken pieces, made a new soul out of me,
I was a prisoner in captivity, but Jesus set me free.... Amen

SAVED

It's like trying to count the grains of sand
that are scattered on the beach,
When your aiming for a target that you know you'll never reach.
But thankfully the Lord above, does not ask for perfection,
But only that we follow Him, and He will give direction.

So, put away all thoughts you hold that you're not good enough,
Never let your mind deceive that the going is too tough.
And don't be so misguided, that you've wandered way too far,
You only have to call on Him and He'll accept you as you are.

There's a choice that lies in front of us, and soon we must decide,
For soon He's coming back again, there'll be no place left to hide.
And knowing I belong to Him, my very heart that calms,
Will you be found among the goats, or rescued with the lambs?

For the price of sin has been redeemed, there's nothing left to pay,
And I will be among the saved, when comes that Glorious day.
I only hope you'll stand with me to welcome His return.
So, the fires in Hell will be put out, with
no souls left to burn.... Amen.

EASTER

Hope was all abandoned and the World was left distraught,
But we never should have doubted you, after everything you taught.
For we could not know the outcome, as they nailed you to that cross
As all we felt was emptiness at this moment of our loss.

You claimed you were the Son of God; we believed all that you said
So, how in spite of all you told, could we believe you dead.
But the game was not yet finished, there was one more card to play,
For in three days you returned again, when the stone was rolled away.

And our faith was all rewarded, and our trust in you repaid,
When you overcame the scourge of death, exactly as you said.
Your resurrection stands as proof, if any is required,
That the Son of Man was all He said and all that we desired.

And so, you snatched a victory, from the jaws of such defeat,
And because our Saviour's still alive the victory was so sweet.
The blood you shed was not in vain, but purchased all our sin,
For there's a tomb outside Jerusalem, that no-
one dwells within.... Amen.

PROTECTOR

When adversity surrounded me, it was you who eased my fears,
When no-one seemed to be around, it was you who caught my tears.
When storms were gathering overhead, it was you who sheltered me,
When I was weak you shielded me, from every enemy.

You provided me with armour, and kept me from all harm,
When danger froze me in my tracks, you offered up your arm.
And though the battle raged around me,
it could neither kill nor maim,
For I carry the flag of Jesus, and my standard bears His name.

So, for all the times I needed you and you were always there,
For all the times I spoke with you, and you answered every prayer.
There is truly no-one like you Lord, it's essential that I tell,
I'm indebted to my Saviour, who looks after me so well.... Amen.

THE HOLY BOOK

If we take things out of context, it's a dangerous game to play,
For words can then be twisted into things we didn't say.
We must also pay attention to the words we're writing down,
For a comma or a question mark, can turn things all around.

But I thank God for His promise, on which I have relied,
That cannot be disputed, in spite of those who've tried.
I thank Him for His Holy Book and the truth that it contains,
That other books have come and gone, But His word still remains.

And so, I trust each word I read, that's written in His book,
For His wisdom's there for all to see, you only have to look.
Each and every word recorded, say exactly what they mean,
From Genesis to Revelation, and all that's in between.

Though none of us are perfect, no matter how we try,
I believe His words' the manual, that we should all live by.
So, chapter after chapter. let's absorb and take it in,
And live as He intended, for there's many hearts to win.... Amen

AGE

Age is just a number not a sentence, time
is not as crucial as it appears,
It seems like only yesterday we were youthful, but
the days and weeks so quickly turn to years.
It's not important when we give our life to Jesus,
so never think your lifestyle doesn't suit,
As long as we're prepared to hear His message, it
doesn't matter if we're a veteran or recruit.

For in the knowledge we've received the Lords forgiveness,
we're free of all our sin and our mistakes,
He'll accept us without age a consideration, and
what a difference to a life He makes.
So no matter if your still a kid at college, or
regardless if your hair has turned to grey,
It's not too late to take the Lord as Saviour, and
be certain he will not turn you away.

It may be that you've never owned a Bible, or can
recite all of the scriptures of by heart,
Each and everyone of us are precious, rest
assured that everyone can play a part.
Jesus holds the key to true salvation, for He told
us He's the life, the truth, the way,
Everyone who asks will be forgiven, whether you
have known Him years or just today....Amen.

FOR ETHIOPIA

I went to Ethiopia not knowing what I'd find,
But what I witnessed over there, keeps playing on my mind,
I saw the children barefoot as they made their way to school,
I thought I knew what poverty was, but wasn't I the fool.

And even after I returned to comfort once again,
I thought of things that I could do, to try and ease their pain,
The memories of the things I'd seen, resurfaced now and then,
But all I had to offer was some paper and a pen.

So I spread a page in front of me, and I began to write,
And words I'd never used before, kept coming into sight,
Rhymes began to formulate, the words sent from above,
And a book of poems did soon appear, with words born out of love.

And I sit here six books later, thankful each book turned out fine,
But the words were sent from God above, not a single one was mine.
All I did was write them down, and trust they'd pass the test,
For I put my pen to paper and my Saviour did the rest.....Amen.

REBORN

I'm so grateful for that moment, when you called me and I came,
Removed me out of bondage, and took away my shame.
It was the second I gained freedom, as the grey skies turned to blue,
When I waved goodbye to all I was, and welcomed in the new.

The looks I have are similar, my appearance just the same,
My voice has never changed, and there's no difference in my name.
But the change is on the inside, where no-one else can see,
For when the hand of Jesus touched me, I became a different me.

I still have far to travel and I still have much to do,
But Jesus grants me strength, to see the transformation through.
From a sinner who was burdened, to a child who's been set free,
If you care to look much closer then perhaps you'll also see.

The sin I used to carry, by Jesus blood was washed away,
The bill I owed was paid upon the cross that awful day.
The price was oh so heavy, But He paid it just the same,
It was I who was the guilty one, yet He took all the blame.....Amen.

PROVIDER

If they took all my possessions and laid them in a line,
And asked me to identify the most precious one of mine.
Without hesitation, I couldn't fail to point it out,
It's the love that Jesus gives me, and there is no room for doubt.

Take away the rest of them, they do not mean a thing,
Just leave me with my Saviour's love, and I'll have everything,
Gold and Silver tarnish us, and just instil more greed,
But the sustenance we find in God, is all we'll ever need.

He gilds the lilies in the field and covers them in gold,
The beauty that we see in them is something to behold.
He feeds all creatures great and small, and keeps them in His care,
Both the fish that fill the oceans and the birds that fill the air.

For all are His creations, and it's His love that gets us by,
He thought so much of all of us, He sent His Son to die.
With my Provider and Protector, I can face what lies in store,
And as long as He abides in me, I won't need any more.....Amen.

COME

If you haven't yet met Jesus, for fear you won't fit in,
I wonder who you turn to, if anguish should begin.
If you've never found a Saviour, who will listen to you call,
I wonder who you pray to, or if you do at all.

If your living in seclusion, believing life holds nothing more,
With every day that passes, exactly like the one before,
If it seems your treading water, yet you're getting nowhere fast,
Just counting down the minutes, til the day you breathe your last.

Surely you must recognise, there's more to life than this,
If your life's a mere existence, then there's something quite amiss.
Send a prayer to Jesus, the one who paid your bill,
When that hole is growing deeper, just know it's only He can fill,

In Him you'll find a purpose, a reason to go on,
You'll find a friend who'll stand by you, when the others are all gone.
A Provider and Protector, a Forgiver of your sin,
Come today, He's waiting, so your new life can begin...Amen.

GLORIOUS DAY

Pushing through the barriers that life puts in my way,
Grateful that my Lord above has given me this day.
Another day to serve Him, for all He's given me,
To thank Him for the Son He sent, who's blood has set me free,

I rise to meet the morning, wipe the sleep from out my eyes,
I look towards the Heavens, and I thank Him for this prize,
For loving me, protecting me, with every step I take,
For feeling His forgiveness, after each of my mistakes.

I serve a worthy Master, who will forever reign,
He's shown how much He cares for me, time and time again.
I know He's there to listen, each and every time I call,
I am humble in His presence for He's sovereign over all.

And when I come to meet Him, I'm unsure how I'll react,
For all I have I owe to Him, I know that for a fact,
Perhaps I'll bow before Him, or fall down at His feet,
But what a Glorious day to come, that day we get to meet....Amen.

JESUS CHANGES LIVES

I can see you're far from happy, by those tears that fill your eyes,
For no matter how you camouflage, your tears you can't disguise.
I only wish I understood, what's caused you so much grief,
Then maybe I could point the way, that offers you relief.

Life can be so troublesome, if your living it alone,
Gazing all your waking hours at a silent telephone.
There's none to share that heartache, that you carry deep inside,
It's like standing at the altar, knowing your a jilted bride.

Have you given thought to Jesus, in your moments of despair,
You only have to call His name, and He'll be waiting there.
I know He feels your anguish, and I know He shares your pain,
When life has thrown you to the ground, He'll help you rise again.

You'll find a friend in Jesus, and He won't let you down,
He'll shoulder all your burdens, and turn your life around,
Search and you will find Him, He can make a weak man strong,
You'll find He's just a prayer away, and has been all along...Amen.

MY THANKS

For every breath I'm taking Lord, I send my thanks to you,
For every hurdle that I face, I know you'll bring me through,
When I am down you lift me up, to a bright and fairer place,
When I am weak you grant me strength, by the power of your Grace.

You catch the bitter tears I shed, if I should ever cry,
You wrap your arms around me Lord, and always wipe them dry.
I feel your presence all around, you keep the wolves at bay,
You lend an ear to listen Lord, and hear each word I say.

It may well be I could survive, not knowing you at all,
But who'd be there to lift me up, every time I fall.
For I would be the loser, should I turn your love away,
I need to feel your presence Lord, more and more each day.

And I thank you for that precious blood, that washed away my sin,
So when my life on Earth is through, a new one will begin,
In that place that you have promised me,
where tears cannot be found,
And I will spend Eternity, with you, on Holy Ground....Amen.

HOW ABOUT YOU?

Have you kept your Faith a secret, is it safely locked away,
And only when it's needed does it see the light of day.
Do you offer thanks to Jesus, and give the praise He's due,
For the blood He shed, and life He gave, was all for me and you.

Do you ask Him for forgiveness, do you take the time to pray,
Or do other things take precedence and prayer gets in the way.
Do you read the Holy Bible, and acknowledge all it says,
Don't you realise we're unworthy and we have to mend our ways.

Are your Sundays somehow different, do you act a different way,
Don't you believe we need the Lord, each and every day.
Will you praise Him in the morning, and
as each evening's growing dim,
For every day, we have to try, and be much more like Him.

So many awkward questions, I'm sure that you agree,
But these are just a sample of the things that bother me.
I believe that every one of us, owes Jesus so much more,
For He gave His life believing, sin was well worth dying for....Amen.

PREPARE

The weather's unpredictable, no two days are the same,
But we know that when the sky turns grey, it signals there'll be rain.
And when we see a clear blue sky, the Sun will soon appear,
And the roar of thunder lets us know the storm is drawing near.

So there are signs to let us know just what we can expect,
Yet there's also lots of signs around that many just neglect,
The things we witness all around, like war and death and pain,
Just indicate we need to see, Lord Jesus come again.

He told us He was coming back, and now we see the signs,
It's time to place your trust in Him, we're running out of time.
He told us He's returning, like a thief into the night,
And everything we see today, convinces me He's right.

Take a look around you and you'll see just what I mean,
Greed and selfishness abounds, all out there to be seen.
We need you our Lord Jesus, like we've never done before,
We're ready now to welcome you, this world
can't take much more....Amen.

GRANDMA'S BIBLE

I remember Grandma's Bible, like it was yesterday,
And how she used to fetch it all those times I came to stay
She would sit back in her rocking chair, while I sat at her knee,
And all those stories that she told, that fascinated me.

I remember how her voice was frail, and she would often cry,
But still that sparkle never failed to light up both her eyes.
Her fingers gently turned each page, as I grew more amazed,
I never dared to interrupt, that's the way that I was raised.

And as each chapter finished, I would beg her for some more,
And She'd give in, to my request, 'til her fingers got too sore.
So then she'd set the Bible down, and start to question me,
On every verse that she had read, 'til Mum came with our tea.

And when it came our time for bed, at the ending of the day,
We'd both kneel down together, and solemnly we'd pray.
I wish I could have Grandma back, to once again enjoy,
That time we spent together, my Grandmother and her boy....Amen.

DAVID'S STORY

David was a skinny kid who was bullied while at school,
Jim McClure by far the worst, a bully and a fool.
But all the other kids in class, made life a living hell,
So much so, he prayed each day, until he heard the bell.

But as the years went rolling by, David soon was saved.
He gave his life to Jesus, it was something that he'd craved,
And then he started preaching, and hundreds came to hear,
He filled each place where he appeared,
they came from far and near.

And then an opportunity, when God unlocked a door.
He got to speak at the little church, he was always longing for.
The church he went to as a kid, where he first met the Lord,
And a loyal servant of his King, was given his reward.

They came from every walk of life, to hear young David speak,
The congregation seated down, so David took a peek.
He may have been mistaken, but now was pretty sure,
That among the crowd who came to hear,
was bully Jim McClure...Amen.

THE GAME OF CHESS

Each decision that we make is like a game of chess,
Good ones leave us satisfied, but bad ones in a mess.
It's easy making up our minds, when the answer's cut and dry,
But sometimes we just can't decide no matter how we try.

We're bound to make the odd mistake, of that I'm pretty sure,
Even when we've based our choice, with intentions that are pure,
In every game there's winners, but there's also losers too,
So ask yourself the question, which of them are you?

If you haven't yet decided, to come to Jesus Christ,
When your time of Earth is at an end, you'll pay a heavy price.
Consider Jesus offer, tell me how can you refuse,
When Eternity's within your grasp, and there's nothing you can lose.

Yes life is like a game of chess, from the moment that we're born.
Have you progressed to King or Queen, or are you still a pawn?
The game will be decided, when we reach that Judgement day,
Find checkmate living for the Lord, there is no other way..Amen.

SHINE

The light within my heart's because of Jesus,
for I realise there is no other name,
It's up to me to try to seek out others, and draw
them like a moth towards His flame,
There are many souls out there that need Him
badly, lives are getting darker every day,
And I must be the beacon that attracts them, like a
lighthouse glowing bright to show the way.

I must radiate in every passing moment, so the
light in me can penetrate the dark,
I must search for souls in every darkened corner, or
the future that they face may well be stark.
For maybe Satan has them in his clutches, And
captured them with sheer dishonesty,
Then the light in me may give them new direction,
and bring them to the place they yearn to be.

Jesus told us we should be disciples, to go
into the world and spread the news,
Never hide your light beneath a bushel, always
be forthcoming with your views.
The flame within my heart keeps burning brighter,
by now it's so much brighter than the Sun,
I pray the Lord I serve will keep it burning, 'til I Ie
has won the soul of everyone...Amen.

FORGIVE

People that we love can sometimes hurt us, and
deep inside our anger starts to swell,
But if we're really honest with each other, That
anger that we feel hurts us as well.
It builds and builds inside us like a cancer, until
we feel that we can take no more,
And the longer that we fail to see the danger,
then it starts to fester like an open sore,

But there's a way to overcome the heartache,
that arguments keep leaving at our door,
The answer's found in having true forgiveness,
when you can't take the torment any-more.
It takes a lot of courage when we're angry, but
that's where Jesus Christ will lend a hand,
When all around opinions are divided, Jesus never fails to understand.

He taught us when He dwelt in human body, That
His Father will reward us when we're meek,
If we're prepared to follow His example, and
always try to turn the other cheek.
No-one ever said it would be easy, but He will
grant you all the strength you need,
And if you find the going gets to heavy, that's
when you will find He'll intercede

285

Bobbie Greer

Words of anger only bring division, and once
their spoken can't be taken back,
If we could be a little more like Jesus, but
sadly it's His patience that we lack,
Yet if we ask, I know He's there to help us, His
hand is there to help us when we try,
Send a prayer and hand it all to Jesus, then count
to ten and let things pass you by...Amen.

NONE BUT JESUS

No-one thought to take my hand or ask me how I felt,
No-one heard my heartfelt plea, as by my bed I knelt.
No-one saw the tears I shed, the ones I covered well,
They only saw the mask I wore, so they could never tell.

Whenever I say no-one, that's not strictly true
For there was one who saw it all, the only one that knew,
The one who witnessed all my pain, and every tear that fell,
The one I told in confidence, and knew He wouldn't tell.

When I thought I was unworthy, He told me differently,
He helped me overcome the grief and saw the best in me.
When I was left abandoned, with no place left to hide,
He told me He was with me, and would never leave my side.

He's my guardian and teacher, my confident and friend,
The one I always turn to, with love beyond an end.
The one who gave His life for me, and paid the asking price,
The one who gave me hope again, My Saviour Jesus Christ....Amen.

THE DOORWAY

Death is but a doorway, from which we cannot hide,
And we can only speculate, what's on the other side.
Some believe it's Paradise, and others that it's Hell,
But the truth is when we reach that door, it's only then we'll tell.

Some believe that when we die, there's no door to be found,
They bury us and then we simply wither in the ground,
But have they heard of Jesus Christ, who bought our liberty,
Who gave His life on Calvary's cross for our Eternity.

This life is just a stepping stone to the one that lies ahead,
To that place prepared and waiting, just like Jesus said,
It's how we choose to live our lives, that underlines our fate,
Accept the Lord while you have time, before it gets too late.

And when you stand before that door, and it slowly opens wide,
Our Saviour will be waiting there to welcome you inside.
And because of how you trusted Him and
your Faith in Him was strong,
It's then you'll find His promises were truthful all along...Amen.

MEMORIES

Photographs can capture precious moments,
with images as sharp as any knife,
They signpost in a way that's almost magic, for
it's memories that constitute a life.
We can look back on events that really shaped us,
and turned us to the person that we are,
We can see how age has quickly crept upon us,
and how each wound has left us with a scar.

But it is really fair that we look backwards, for
we can't change the things already done,
Perhaps it would be better to look forward, to the
times that lie ahead that's yet to come.
For every passing day that we are given, is another
day that God has passed our way,
So ask yourself if you have made provision, and
are ready should He call you home today.

Have you come to terms that we won't live forever,
at least not in the way we did before,
We need to make our peace with God our Maker,
and be prepared for what may lie in store.
The years that we've been given mount so quickly,
and those photographs will slowly start to fade,
But the Kingdom of the Lord goes on forever, so we
should focus minds on this instead...Amen.

FOR VICKY

I know the storm I face won't last forever, and
I realise there's better times ahead,
But for now I feel the world upon my shoulders,
as I stand and stare at you beside this bed,
And now I see your pain I feel so guilty, despite
how others say I'm not to blame,
If only I had been more understanding, perhaps
I wouldn't carry so much shame.

The doctors say the signs are getting better, it's
this that keeps me going for a while,
But just to have you back to how I know you,
to see again that enigmatic smile.
The pressure that you faced was so enormous,
and I feel I didn't carry my fair share.
If only I had listened more intently, so when
you called on me I would be there.

For now my love I only have a promise, that
I'll try to be the best that I can be,
I'll try to fill the spaces that were missing, if
only Jesus gives you back to me.
We aways take the one we love for granted,
it's only now I see that to be true,
I'm sorry for my selfishness apparent, and for
never being a better friend to you.

Life has taught me many different lessons, but
Jesus always brought me through the fight,
And I know that He will lay His hand upon you,
as sure as daytime follows every night.
I also feel His presence all around you, every time I visit at your bed,
And our Faith in Him will bring us both together, to
those happy times that's waiting just ahead...Amen.

THE FRIEND

When tear-drops feel like acid, and really start to burn,
There's a friend who offers comfort, asking nothing in return.
When a heart is badly broken, or a life is in despair,
There's a friend we can depend on, the one who's ever there.

When we need a hand of healing, when hope is almost gone,
There's a miracle available from that friend we call upon.
When you've used up all your laughter, and forgotten how to smile,
There's a friend who'll build a bridge for
you to make your life worthwhile.

Who's this friend I talk about, and where can He be found,
The one who's promised to remove the chains that have me bound.
Seek and you will find Him. He's never far away,
He'll listen to your every word if you take the time to pray.

A life can be rebuilt again, and hope can be restored,
Speak with Him in times of need for no-one is ignored.
You'll know Him by the scars He bears, because of Calvary's shame,
When all else fails, just turn to Him for Jesus is His name...Amen.

STEADFAST

Opinions sometimes differ, and arguments ensue,
It may well be the views I hold are not the same as you.
If all of us could just agree, but that may never be,
But I hold unto the principal that truth will set you free.

Promises get broken, sometimes minds are changed,
Positions sometimes fluctuate and lives are re-arranged.
Yet the only thing that's constant, steadfast in every way,
Is the word of God He gave to us, so relevant to-day.

His word's the Rock of Ages, to which I'll always cling,
All else moves like drifting sand, and I mean everything.
But the God we have is mighty yet full of good intention,
Capable of miracles beyond our comprehension.

Fashions tend to fade away, and tides may ebb and flow,
But the word of God is permanent, like nothing else I know.
His truth remains unflinching, throughout the passing years,
The promises He's gave and kept, sweet music to my ears...Amen.

HIS MERCY

We offered prayers to Heaven, and Jesus must have heard,
For He reached down and touched you, to demonstrate He cared.
I suppose He really knew you, and saw you as His own,
His touch has brought you back to me, so I am not alone.

My Faith in Him rewarded, my Trust in Him renewed,
I bow and give my thanks to Him, the way I know I should.
By His Mercy I can live again, I've overcome the pain,
He saw how much I needed you and brought you back again.

I won't forget how much He's done, no matter where I roam,
For the God I serve is worthy, and He has brought you home.
The darkest days by now have passed, New light begins to shine,
All is well because of Him, Almighty God of mine...Amen.

THE OLD SOLDIER

His head was full of memories, of far off battlefields,
For war is like an open sore that never really heals.
The glamour's left to Hollywood, where no-one really dies,
But the thought of all the friends he lost, brings tears to both his eyes.

He doesn't like to mention it, the pain too much to share,
And you wouldn't really understand, because you were not there.
These fields that look so tranquil now, where grass conceals the mud,
But back when he remembered them, were
stained with soldiers blood.

He often thinks of those now gone, who didn't make it home,
And asks why he was different, in the hours he spends alone.
Was it really through the will of God, that luck was on his side,
That He survived the Hell on Earth, when many others died.

But he takes his consolation, believing God had brought him through,
And every day he makes the time to give the thanks he's due.
He may be a worn out soldier, with some medals on his chest,
But every day he thanks the Lord, for how
much he's been blessed...Amen

THE LIFE TO COME

Someday when the toils of life are over, and I
lay my burdens down at Jesus feet.
I will look into His eyes in sheer amazement,
then bow before Him at the Mercy seat.
And all the weight that I was forced to carry, that
heavy load that life has made me bear,
Will be lifted in an instant from my shoulders,
and disappear like it was never there.

These eyes of mine that once saw things so clearly,
but age has took its toll and made them dim,
Will be once again restored to perfect vision,
when I receive a single touch from Him.
The weariness that's held me as a prisoner, will
melt away as snow beneath the Sun,
As joy replaces all my disappointments, this will
happen when my new life has begun.

So I don't count the days the way I used to,
death no longer holds me in its grip,
I know the Lord I love is holding firmly, and I
know that from His hand I'll never slip.
Every day that passes brings me closer, to that
place that Jesus Christ has promised me,
Where I will get to dwell among the Angels, and
there with Him I'll spend Eternity....Amen.

GODS PLAN

As long as I have Jesus, I've ample strength in store,
For He laid down His life for me, and who could ask for more.
If I'm knocked down one hundred times,
He'll bring me through the pain,
He'll lift me to my feet once more, and I will rise again.

Tomorrow may bring sorrow, but I'll retain my trust,
Storms may gather overhead, I know at times they must.
But through the darkest Winter, there'll be no need to hide,
My shelter's found in Jesus, knowing He is by my side.

The will of God takes precedence, above the aims of Man,
There may be times it's difficult, for us to understand,
But even in our darkest hour our trust must be the key,
For God has set a plan in place, and that's how things will be.

It's good to know the God I serve, is there and in control,
Shattered lives have been repaired, and broken hearts made whole.
We have a God who's merciful, who I am proud to serve,
With the Blessings that He pours on me,
much more than I deserve...Amen.

STAY

You satisfy the needs in me, in every passing hour,
Compassionate in every way, that's just the way you are.
You always come in search of me, and never fail to find,
You ease this aching heart of mine and grant me peace of mind.

Don't ever let me lose you Lord, for that I couldn't bear,
For life's not worth the living, if it means that your not there.
If I should lose my Tower of Strength, I couldn't bear the cost,
Your love is irreplaceable, I couldn't take the loss,

So always keep your promise Lord that you'll abide with me,
That where one or two are gathered Lord, there you'll always be.
Let me feel your presence in every hour of every day,
Promise you won't leave me Lord, that you are here to stay.

For all I have I owe to you, so promise you won't leave
Your the blood that's pumping through me
veins, the very air I breathe,
You give me strength to face each day, my love for you has grown,
And I know I wouldn't make it Lord, if I were left alone...Amen.

FOUND

Was it fate or just by accident that I discovered you?
Or perhaps you came and called to me,
when you felt the time was due.
No matter what the circumstance, I'm glad it came to pass,
It may have took a little while, but I've found you at last.

And oh how great the change I feel, now that I walk with you,
I've overcame the loneliness and hardships I once knew.
The pillow that I slept upon, was wet from tears I cried,
Yet I only had to call on you, but you let me decide.

Your arms were always waiting there, to offer an embrace,
With a gentle hand so willing to dry those tears that stained my face
But above all with forgiveness for all my sin and crime,
I was falling but you reached to me and caught me just in time.

When I look back, it's with regret, I never felt the need,
To come to you Lord Jesus Christ, so you could intercede.
But in the end I found you Lord, or maybe you found me.
You taught me how to live again, and a sinner was set free...Amen.

HE LIVES

"Jesus is returning" and how my heart delights,
It should be written ten feet tall, in coloured neon lights.
Why keep it a secret, why keep it subdued,
Tell the world He's coming back and spread the glorious news.

Shout it from the rooftops, let everybody hear,
He told us He'd return again, and now the time is near.
Look towards the Heavens, with gladness in your heart,
See the Son of God return, as clouds begin to part.

Angels in attendance, adorned in robes of white,
A heavenly procession, oh what a marvellous sight.
He's coming for His children, to show them how He's cared,
To lead them to those mansions, that's already been prepared.

Yes, Jesus is returning, no matter what they say,
Watch the skies, you never know, today might be that day.
And all the world will bow to Him, and acknowledge Him as King,
The one who died yet lives again, how that
makes my heart sing...Amen.

BELIEVE

I believe there is a Heaven and it's everything it seems,
A place that's indescribable, beyond our wildest dreams.
And I believe I'll get there, when my days on Earth are through,
For Jesus made a promise and I believe it to be true.

I believe in God above, who knows our every thought,
Who sent His Son to die for me, so forgiveness could be bought.
And I believe He walked again, Oh what a Glorious day,
Whenever Angels came to Earth and rolled the stone away.

And I believe He's coming back, the way the Bible's told,
To lead us back to Heaven where the streets are paved with gold.
And then the World will get to see His prophesy come true.
These are things that I believe, I wonder do you too....Amen.

RESCUED

What a timely intervention Jesus made on my behalf,
I'd forgotten how it felt to smile, and forgotten how to laugh.
I was reaching out to find a friend, but they were out of range,
But suddenly He touched me, and my life began to change.

I was looking in wrong places for the answer to my call,
For a bottle or a needle didn't really help at all.
They just prolonged the misery, til I awoke next day,
But they didn't make the heartaches or the problems go away.

Then along came Jesus, when I needed Him so much,
I asked if He could help me and He answered with a touch,
He didn't have to do it, but He gave it out of love,
I was looking in the gutter when the answer lay above.

So thank you to my Saviour, who listened to my plea,
The only one who's capable of saving one like me.
When I was crying out for help, He heard me loud and clear,
He bought me to my feet again, when no-
one else could hear...Amen.

HEAVEN'S GAIN

Heaven gained another Star that day you went away,
I know you've found a better place, but I miss you anyway.
My world seems so much smaller, and time just drags along,
But I know we'll get to meet again, in that place we both belong.

The suffering is over, your now at perfect peace,
The Lord has shown you mercy, and has given you release.
But in truth I really miss you, for my life is not the same,
Yet for us to be with Jesus, that's the nature of the game.

I keep your photo by my bed, it helps to ease the pain,
I say good-night before I sleep, time and time again,
And each and every morning when I open up my eyes,
I see you smiling back at me, as I'm about to rise.

What a day we're going to have, when my day does arrive,
For the flame of love I hold for you is very much alive.
We'll meet again at Heavens gates, where I'll lift you aloft,
The Lord will re-unite us, to pick up where we left off...Amen.

THE THIRD DAY

When we hear the name of Jesus, we think of Calvary,
Where the Son of God laid down His life for the sin of you and me.
We think of all that suffering, and the pain that He endured,
But its only through His sacrifice that hope could be assured.

So should we be pre-occupied or let our memories stray?
To what occurred at Josephs tomb, that glorious third day.
It was then we tasted Victory, after all that grief and pain,
When we heard our Saviour was alive and Jesus walked again.

Yes, Calvary was tragic, in oh so many ways,
And it's only right it lives with us until the end of days,
But don't forget the victory, that was waiting in the wings,
For they couldn't take away the life, of our Almighty King of Kings,

So never forget Calvary, the hillside or the Cross,
But please remember how He won when we thought the battle lost.
Remember we've a living God, who's Kingdom will endure,
While those of Men all fade away, The Lords will be secure....Amen.

THE WEDDING PLAN

The Wedding plans were all in place down to the finest thing,
The cars were booked, the cake was baked,
the Groom had bought the ring.
Every detail catered for, there was nothing overlooked,
The Church was ready for the day, the Honeymoon all booked.

Such a lot of planning to ensure that all went well,
Every angle covered, down to who would ring the bell.
The vows would soon be taken, with promises exchanged,
A newly married couple who's lives were re-arranged.

With their future spread before them, exactly how God meant,
But all of this took planning and didn't come by accident.
And when the day is over, and confetti's all be thrown,
I wonder will they plan ahead, for when one of them's alone.

We need to plan for eternity, for there's none of us can tell,
Tomorrow isn't promised, we must plan for it as well.
For death can separate us, but while in the Lord we trust,
Our spirit goes to Glory while our bodies turn to dust....Amen.

Bobbie Greer

WORDS

While God keeps sending words to me, I will write them down,
And trust when others read them, that the needs in them are found.
Let Jesus be the author, and I will be the scribe,
With pen in hand I'll Honour Him, without reward or bribe.

The power of words in every sense, more powerful than the sword,
And just to know they've touched someone, let that be my reward.
I'll try to capture every word that Jesus sends to me,
In the hope that something that I write, will set another free.

Others facing problems, that may well be severe,
May read my words and understand that help is standing near.
It only takes a word or two, and He will hear your plight,
He'll lift your spirits, touch your heart, and make things seem alright.

I only ask you take the time, if you would be so kind.
To give some thought to what I've said and then make up your mind.
I'll always do my very best to relate what I've been told,
As long as words are given, and Jesus has me in His hold...Amen.

Lightning Source UK Ltd.
Milton Keynes UK
UKHW012219210220
359134UK00003B/138

9 781984 593962